Heinrich Döll's sketch for the second act in the first production (Munich, 1865)

This Opera Guide is sponsored by

Tristan & Isolde

Richard Wagner

Opera Guide Series Editor: Nicholas John

Calder Publications Limited
Riverrrun Press Inc.
Paris · London · New York

Published in association with English National Opera

COPYRIGHT DATA

First published in Great Britain, 1981, by Calder Publications Limited 9-15 Neal Street, London WC2H 9TU

First published in the U.S.A., 1981, by Riverrun Press Inc., 1170 Broadway, New York, NY 10001

BRITISH LIBRARY CATALOGUING IN PUBLICATION DATA
Wagner, Richard, *1813-1883*
　Tristan and Isolde.—(English National Opera Guides; 6)
　1. Wagner, Richard, *1813-1883*. Tristan and Isolde
　2. Operas—Librettos
　I. John, Nicholas　　II. Wagner　　III. Series
　782.1'092'4　　ML310.W14

ISBN 0-7145-3849-3

English National Opera receives financial assistance from the Arts Council of Great Britain.

Typeset in Plantin by Spooner Typesetting & Graphics, London NW5.

CONTENTS

LIST OF ILLUSTRATIONS

Cover design by Rupert Kirby
Frontispiece: Heinrich Döll's sketch for the second act in the first production (Munich 1865)

figuratively speaking, be a Senta to his wandering, storm-tossed Dutchman, a saintly Elizabeth to his Tannhäuser, the sublime *Ewig-Weibliche* (eternal in Woman), described by Goethe, who would elevate and redeem the Faust in him. The music and drama of *The Flying Dutchman* and *Tannhäuser*, particularly, paved the way for *Tristan*.

Like so many of the Romantics, Wagner's eroticism was highly developed, and was reflected even in his earliest operatic attempts. It was an aspect of his music which Victorian critics found too vivid and unrestrained. Tannhäuser fluctuated between sensual indulgence to the point of boredom in the Venusberg, and aspirations towards a love for Elizabeth that was purer and more permanent. It was only after completing *Tristan* that Wagner felt able, in 1860, to reinforce the erotic music for the Venusberg scene in the new *Tristan* idiom, almost burlesquing it in places, for the Paris production of *Tannhäuser*.

The hero of this work only achieved salvation after his death, and through the sacrificial death of the saintly Elizabeth. Similarly, Wagner's Dutchman could only be released from his eternal wanderings and curse, by the sacrificial love of Senta, and after their deaths, their spiritual bodies are seen united, rising heavenwards out of the sea. It was no coincidence that, while toying with the idea of a work based on the Tristan legend, he should be reflecting on his *Flying Dutchman* score, and that he subsequently gave the last pages a cadence of redemptive transfiguration in the style of Isolde's *Verklärung*. It is interesting to remember that in his original 1848 'Sketch' for what later became *The Ring* cycle, Wagner had continued this theme of redemption, and the triumph of love over death: the figures of the dead Siegfried and Brünnhilde were to be resurrected from the funeral pyre, and be seen ascending to a redeemed Valhalla.

The blossoming of the musical style of the love drama of *Tristan and Isolde* was inevitable, as part of Wagner's very rapid stylistic development, and it received a stimulus (not, as romantic writers would have it, inspiration) from a love affair with Mathilde Wesendonck*. He met her and her husband Otto in Switzerland in 1853, and they became his devoted admirers and close friends. Enraptured by his *Tannhäuser* music, Mathilde was already falling in love with him, and, in responding, Wagner soon found himself deeply involved. When the Wesendoncks built a palatial villa outside Zurich, they provided a cottage nearby for Richard and Minna, which he named 'Asyl' (Refuge). He walked across nearly every day to play Mathilde his composition sketches. The Wesendonck villa soon attracted many other artists and intellectuals, with Wagner as its dominating star. Minna felt hopelessly out of her depth. She did not know that Wagner's affair was condoned, albeit with some reluctance, by Otto, who was prepared to accept his wife's claim that it served an artistic purpose. Mathilde believed totally in Wagner's genius, and provided a sympathetic spirit that was his real 'refuge'.

In 1854 he dedicated the Prelude of *The Valkyrie* to her, and inscribed abbreviated tributes to her in the score of the Act One duet. His need for love was then released into the music of the doomed Siegmund and Sieglinde, and into Wotan's Farewell. The first Act had introduced something into *The Ring* cycle, something so far lacking: a purely human love story, and the musician's imagination blazed up to produce a symphonic outpouring of wonderful music, in a different style from *Rheingold*. He now looked for a story where he could develop this type of love music throughout an entire drama.

When he wrote the letter to Liszt which heads this essay, he had depicted in

* They spelt the name with a 'ck' although their son later dropped the 'c'.

10

Synopsis

Timothy McFarland

The opera is set in the legendary Celtic world of the early Middle Ages. Many significant events have taken place before it begins, and are recounted at various points in the work, particularly by Isolde in her long account to Brangäne in the first act. These events make up about half the story in Wagner's main source, the courtly romance *Tristan* by Gottfried von Strassburg (c. 1210), and the composer simplified the complex narrative, telescoping episodes and reducing the number of persons, when preparing his text.

Tristan, a Breton nobleman, has left his ancestral home Kareol to serve his uncle, King Mark of Cornwall. He established his position at court and was adopted by Mark as his heir after defeating and slaying Morold, an Irish knight who had forced Cornwall to pay tribute. Morold's severed head had been mockingly sent back to Ireland as 'tribute', but it contained a splinter from the victor's sword, and Tristan himself has received a wound from Morold's poisoned weapon. The only person who could heal this wound was the Irish princess Isolde, who had sworn to avenge Morold, her betrothed. Tristan therefore assumed the anagrammatical name of 'Tantris' and sailed to Ireland; but Isolde, while tending him, discovered that the splinter from Morold's head matched a notch in Tristan's sword and thus guessed his identity. She immediately resolved to take revenge with the sword that had slain Morold. But when she was about to do so, Tristan opened his eyes and gazed at her—'not at the sword, not at my hand, he gazed in my eyes', and she was unable to do the deed. This episode is of central importance for the opera.

Tristan, healed of his wound, swore 'a thousand oaths of eternal gratitude and loyalty' and returned to Cornwall. There the jealous courtiers urge the widower Mark to remarry, but he refuses to do so until Tristan himself threatens to leave the court forever unless Mark permits him to go and woo Isolde on his behalf, thereby probably disinheriting himself. Mark gives his reluctant consent, and Tristan sails to Ireland once again. The feud between the two countries is solemnly ended and a marriage alliance concluded.

Act One is set on the ship bringing Tristan and Isolde to Cornwall. She tells her maid Brangäne what had happened earlier, expresses her humiliation and rage at Tristan's behaviour, curses him and resolves that they both shall die. She demands of Tristan that they drink 'atonement' and he accepts, comprehending her real intention and tortured by the passion he cannot admit. But Brangäne has substituted a love-potion for the poison, and so, as the ship arrives at Cornwall, Isolde and Tristan find that their love for each other has been released by the potion and that, instead of death together, they are condemned to life with an irresistible and inadmissible love.

In Act Two, Tristan's best friend, Melot, has arranged a hunt at night, ostensibly to give the lovers an opportunity to meet. Brangäne warns Isolde in vain that Melot is treacherous, and the lovers celebrate the night that enables them to reject life itself in a state of mystical union. Brangäne's warnings are disregarded and the lovers are discovered by King Mark and the hunting party. Mark reproaches Tristan for having broken his oaths of loyalty, and once again Tristan seeks death — by throwing himself on Melot's sword.

7

Act Three takes place at Kareol, Tristan's neglected home in Brittany. The faithful Kurwenal has brought him here, mortally wounded, and has sent for Isolde to heal him once again. When the delirious Tristan regains consciousness, he yearns for Isolde and for release from the torment of life; as her arrival is announced, he tears the bandages from his wound and dies in her arms. Mark and Brangäne arrive, bringing understanding and forgiveness too late. Isolde's lament for Tristan is a triumphant apotheosis as she sinks lifeless on to Tristan's body.

Milka Ternina, the Croatian soprano whose 1895 London debut as Isolde opposite Jean de Reszke's Tristan was acclaimed. (Stuart-Liff Collection)

Kirsten Flagstad, the Norwegian soprano, as Isolde at Covent Garden (1936). (Covent Garden Archives)

A Landmark in Musical History

John Luke Rose

As I have never in my life felt the real bliss of love, I must erect a monument to the most beautiful of all my dreams, in which, from beginning to end, that love shall be thoroughly satiated. I have in my head a *Tristan und Isolde*, the simplest, but most full-blooded, musical conception.

Wagner wrote this in a letter to Liszt, of December 16, 1854, but the music drama which eventually emerged was more than 'a monument to ideal love'. It became one of the landmarks of cultural history. The legend on which it is based had been famous far back into the Gothic period; Dante refers to Tristan in *The Divine Comedy* (*Inferno, Canto V*). Whereas Shakespeare, in an equally famous love drama, explores the poetic aspects of tragic adolescent love in *Romeo and Juliet*, Wagner explores all the conscious and unconscious aspects of mature adult love. By excluding all incidental episodes from the legend, he concentrates on the souls of the lovers, illuminating metaphysical as well as erotic aspects of love. This illumination comes, not so much from his poem, as from the unique style of the orchestral music, which evokes, powerfully as well as sensitively, every shade of emotion in all the characters, ranging from mockery, pride and despair, to sublime ecstasy. Wagner's musical inspiration here reached its supreme peak, which he may have equalled in parts of later works, but never surpassed.

Certain biographical incidents need to be considered. As a young man, Richard Wagner fell in love with a pretty actress, Minna Planer, who already had a daughter from one of her earlier affairs. Their marriage was based on shaky foundations; within a few months she had deserted him for another man, but soon returned to her husband. Although for most of their married life she remained physically attractive to him—in his eyes, the Venus to his Tannhäuser—she rarely had faith in his more ambitious creative projects, often scolding him for wasting time in creating unperformable works, when there were plenty of other composers, and when he was already recognised as an outstanding conductor. His theatrical background had made him an incurable spendthrift, and their married life proceeded from one crisis to another: trying to escape from unpaid bills and threatening creditors; near-starvation and imprisonment for debt in Paris in 1840; the Dresden crisis, the 1848–9 Revolution, their flight, abandoning one of Germany's best conducting posts; and so many vital creative years spent in exile, unable to return to Germany, where he was wanted by the police on a charge of treason for his part in the Dresden Revolution. Minna would have had to be a wife of superhuman patience and faith to have endured all this without periodic recriminations—and so she became for him the Fricka to his Wotan, the doubting Elsa to his Lohengrin. Intellectually and spiritually, Richard and Minna were incompatible. He yearned for a being who would share his ideals, and encourage him to higher achievement with womanly compassion. He yearned for something more than physical love, for a woman who would,

The Valkyrie a relationship doomed to tragedy: Siegmund (known as 'Woeful') was, like Tristan, destined for sorrow. It was not until 1857 that the lack of confidence of his publishers, Breitkopf and Härtel, and of possible patrons, convinced Wagner of the impracticability of having his vast *Ring* cycle produced. He sadly abandoned his *Siegfried* score at the end of Act Two, and threw himself into the new work which had for three years been increasingly dominating his thoughts. With an indirect suggestion for an opera commission from the Emperor of Brazil (never confirmed), Wagner foresaw a success. As an exile in Switzerland, he was in great need of money, and he persuaded himself and his publishers that the new work could be performed by any good opera house, and would require only a handful of singers; compared with the forces needed for *The Ring*, it would have a simple plot and scenic demands, and a normal orchestra. Only when he had completed *Tristan and Isolde* in 1859, did he realize that he had made superhuman demands on his two leading singers, in intelligent musicianship, acting and stamina. The 'modest' orchestra emerged as a symphony orchestra to be kept at full stretch for over four hours, with a string section large enough to be divided into many parts.

Between 1854 and 1857, musical ideas had already been jotted down. On June 28, 1857, he wrote to Liszt that he was now 'determined to finish' *Tristan*. He was subconsciously building up the atmosphere and style of the music even before the prose sketch, let alone the final poem, was written. Thus it can be said that none of his works was so truly born out of the spirit of the music. By 1857, now able to act out his fantasies with Mathilde, he felt compelled to develop a drama in which he could make a continuous musical exploration of love. But the result was an artistic achievement far beyond what was inspired by this love affair. His letters to Mathilde are remarkable for their discussion of philosophy as it related to his composition. On stage, in Act Two, the love scene between Tristan and Isolde becomes a similar philosophical discussion—a search for a metaphysical solution, rather than physical satisfaction. Unlike other lovers in life and literature, they do not spend much time in admiring each other's physical features. Their love is not based on the popular concept of outward attractiveness; the lovers might be very plain, and the work would lose nothing of its force in the depiction of profound love.

Wagner's method of composition was to execute a very rough and rapid pencil sketch, and then a much more demanding semi-orchestral one, from which he would make the full orchestral score. When he had completed the last stage for Act One, and the first stage for Act Two, the love affair was over. Mathilde was unwilling to abandon her husband and her children, Wagner to leave his sick wife Minna. The atmosphere of Asyl, where this section of the work was completed, along with his finest songs, *Five Poems of Mathilde Wesendonck* (two of them marked 'Studies for *Tristan and Isolde*'), was already tinged with the melancholy of Minna's possible death. Wagner and Mathilde, absorbed in the philosophy of Schopenhauer and Buddhism, saw the renunciation of their love as the only noble solution, and their relationship gradually returned to the more Platonic friendship from which it had developed, a friendship which both she and Otto maintained until the end of the composer's life in 1883. In 1858 Wagner went to Venice, separating both from Minna (who went for a health cure) and the Wesendoncks. He was now alone with his artistic inspiration, developing the glorious love music of Act Two, and King Mark's soliloquy, which obviously draws upon the composer's own resignation.

For the composition of the remarkable third act, Wagner moved, in March 1859, to a favourite location in Switzerland, Lucerne. The score was completed at the end of the summer, and he then moved to Paris, where Minna joined him in another attempt to resurrect something of their marriage; this later proved impossible, and she died, separated from him, in 1866. *Lohengrin* was making him internationally famous, and such was the publishers' interest in the *Tristan* project, and such was Wagner's own considerable experience, as conductor as well as composer, that while composing Act Two in Venice, he was checking the orchestral proofs of Act One; and similarly checking those of Act Two, while composing Act Three. History proved his confidence fully justified: the tonal balances remain perfect for the style, and the sumptuous sounds of the score, unique. In the first and last parts of the Prelude to Act One, for example, there is frequent use of varied tone-colours, often subtly blended, for either answering or dovetailed phrases in most of the main themes [1, 2, 5, 6, 7 and 8]. In the central development section, they are continually interweaving in melodic lines in separated tone-colours, building to the climax. In the Prelude to Act Three, there are strong contrasts between deep strings [31], high violins [32], the unusual blend of solo cello and horn for the melody of [33] for its first statement, then alternating solo clarinet, oboe and horn, doubling solo viola, for the second statement. One can also observe the expressive use of solo woodwind and horn phrases during Tristan's monologues in this Act and the gorgeous sounds of the C major climax. Richard Strauss described the work's final cadence as the most beautifully orchestrated in all music.

*

The opening quotation comes from a letter in which Wagner described to Liszt his new infatuation with the philosophy of Arthur Schopenhauer, so far ignored in Germany. 'His chief idea, the final negation of the Desire of life, is terribly serious, but it shows the only salvation possible. To me, of course, that thought was not new, and it can, indeed, be conceived by no-one in whom it did not pre-exist, but this philosopher was the first to place it clearly before me. If I think of the storm of my heart, the terrible tenacity with which, against my desire, it used to cling to the hope of life, and if even now I feel this hurricane within me, I have at least found a quietus which, in wakeful nights, helps me to sleep. This is the genuine, ardent longing for death, for absolute unconsciousness, total non-existence. Freedom from all dreams is our only final salvation.' He goes on to mention, significantly in this context, the *Dutchman* score, although here, as in his other works concerned with redemption, there is no 'total non-existence', but a new form of continuity after death. Schopenhauer's teaching is permeated with Indian philosophy, drawn particularly from the Upanishads and from Buddhism. The causes of man's suffering are conceived as a result of endless Desire (symbolized in the opera by theme [2] which is continually developed, from the opening to closing bars). The soul tries to find release from the unending cycle of reincarnation, where what is sown in one life (good or bad deeds) as the result of the Will, produces inevitable consequences in the circumstances of the next lives, according to an immutable law (Karma). The state of conscious freedom from Desire is Nirvana. Mystical aspiration, a calm renunciation of Desire and a willing symbolic 'death' to insatiable craving and to the life of the senses were the essential ingredients of Schopenhauer's lucid and stimulating writings. He felt that, through their 'negation of the Will', great mystics and creative artists, especially musicians, could perceive and express the most

12

Olive Fremstad, the Swedish soprano who made her debut as Isolde at the Met., on the night when Mahler also made his Met. debut.

Lauritz Melchior as Tristan, a painting by Nikol Schattenstein. (Royal Opera House Archives)

profound truths about the essence of being and becoming. Wagner adapted what he felt he needed from these ideas, which are clearly reflected in the symbolic language of the *Tristan* libretto. There is the concept of dualism: life and death, hate and love, Day and Night. For the lovers, from Act Two onwards, Day symbolizes the outer world of vainglory, greed, craving and illusion (similar to the Eastern concept of *maya*), and Wagner's harsh Day theme [16] is constantly developed and transformed in this section. The lovers reject Day for a type of Nirvana consciousness, when they apostrophize comforting, protecting, liberating Night. At this period, Wagner conceived a purely Buddhist drama, *The Victors*, and also contemplated bringing Parzival, the wanderer in search of the Holy Grail, into Act Three of *Tristan*, so that the self-renouncing mystical knight might meet the self-tormenting lover knight. Writing to Mathilde on May 30, 1859, he perceived a close parallel between the third act sufferings of Tristan, and those of Amfortas, and years later, he depicted the latter in a similar chromatic style. As the libretto developed along the lines of Schopenhauer, however,it became unnecessary to introduce Parzival (spelt *Parsifal* in his last music-drama, an individual blend of both Christian and Buddhist symbolism, for which the first prose sketch was written in 1857).

Wagner's poem is written in a very unusual and concentrated style, compared with his previous works. There are many places where a normal poet would need to amplify phrases to give precise definition to the emotions, but which in the opera are left very much to the expressive power of the orchestra. The singers often project their words in sustained tones creating long melodic lines, with few notes against the many in the orchestra. There are unusual psychological and philosophical qualities in the libretto, of unending fascination for discussion. Tristan's attitude to death is a case in point. As a fearless knight ('Death-devoted head!' Isolde describes him, to that impressive theme, [10]), Tristan has often courted death, which holds no fear for him. Both before and during the action, he is critically wounded, needing the famous healing hands of Isolde, and each act produces a similar climax, open to more than one interpretation. In Act One, in a state of wretchedness, he guesses that Isolde offers him poison as atonement, and he gladly accepts it. She has to snatch the cup from him in order to ensure her desired share. At the end of Act Two, at the last moment he changes his mind about revenging himself on the treacherous Melot, and allows his sword to drop, accepting what could have been a fatal wound. In Act Three, he describes how he has already experienced death, hearing its 'door crash behind him', but he has returned to the Daylight world for Isolde. Near the end, driven to the point of madness by pain, longing and despair, the joy of reuniting with Isolde finally unhinges his mind, and he flings off his bandages; he is convinced he no longer needs them, now that she has come to heal the wound, but his rash action proves fatal, and he dies in her arms. The music vividly conveys both his wild joy, and then, in a very moving transition to quieter, slower music, the life ebbing out of him. Isolde sings, finally, not of her grief, but of her vision of a transfigured Tristan, in a form free of all sorrow and suffering, smiling with the joy of love, in a spiritual realm where she is to join him.

The story of Tristan and Isolt (Isolde) has many features typical of a Gothic minstrel's romance: the secret meetings, the faithful friend as lookout, the watch-songs warning the secret lovers of the approach of dawn and possible discovery. The minstrels used to elaborate fanciful details of the intrigues and deceptions practised by the lovers. There were earlier French and Celtic versions of the legend, but Wagner's main source was the 13th century epic poem, *Tristan*, by Gottfried von Strassburg, which he pared down to its essentials, removing the figure of a second Isolde. All the versions, despite a variety of different details, told of a love so intense, that even the physical bodies were a barrier to its ultimate fulfilment, the merging of soul with soul, beyond the cruel limitations of time or the fluctuations of physical passion. The legends concluded with the lovers buried on either side of a chapel. From the tomb of one, grew up a vine; and from the other, a rose (or an ivy), which climbed up an arch, and reached across and intertwined. However often they were cut down, they grew up again and intertwined, and were finally left as a symbol of eternal love.

Wagner reduced the material of the legend, so that he could concentrate on just five main characters, and, with a symphonic continuity unique in opera, he fully explored each emotional situation, and each act progresses towards a major musical and dramatic climax. Apart from the lovers, the other characters only appear in relation to the central situation, but Wagner's characterisation for each of them is equally brilliant, with distinctive musical styles for the bluff, devoted Kurwenal, the sad and introspective King Mark, the watchful Brangäne, and even the small parts, such as the sympathetic yet teasing unaccompanied sailor's song, or the rousing sailors' chorus. The contrasts between all these dramatic elements are always vivid. The Love Potion is preserved from the Gothic legend, employed as something which does not cause, but reveals, true love.

Tristan and Isolde is a very personal artistic expression, embodying a number of clearly defined traits of the Romantic movement. The literary style, as well as the content of his poem, shows, on the one hand, affinities with the works of earlier German Romantics, and on the other, a new type of emotional intensity and psychological realism. His highly concentrated verse aroused the interest of later poets and writers of different countries, including the French symbolists.

*

The score is a landmark in the history of music for a number of reasons. It has a distinctive musical language, with its special harmonic and orchestral colouring. In its use of chromatic linear writing, its instrumental polyphony, free treatment of discords for such periods that the ear finally accepts them almost as concords, *Tristan* was at least fifty years ahead of its time. Compared with his earlier scores, there is a sparing use of brass, apart from the horns, which are regarded more as a part of the woodwind group, and written above the bassoons. They have solo passages throughout, as well as the distant hunting horn effects in Act Two; a distinctive use is also made of hand-muted horn notes and chords. Wagner came to regard the work as the finest embodiment of musico-dramatic theories, in the expressive balance of voices and orchestra in a continuous but often free melodic line, and in 'the art of transition' between sections and dramatic moods. This art of transition he regarded as the supreme challenge for any composer, and was particularly proud of the one in the middle of Act Two, when the lovers' excited exchanges and their heated rejection of the Daylight world, gradually give way to the wonderful music of Night. The shifting emotions of love are potently expressed through the shifting harmonies and orchestral textures, in a small handful of themes continually developed on a symphonic scale. The result is something far more, however, than a symphonic poem with voices. The ebb

15

and flow of extended passages in different tempi and conveying different moods resembles the motion of the sea, which unites and separates the lovers in the legend. The tragic element of the theme of Desire [2] is often conveyed by the darker timbres of oboes and cor anglais, and in a succession of unresolved seventh chords. There are important solo passages for bass clarinet (Mark's lament) and for the cor anglais. The orchestral textures show vividly-imagined detail in every bar, and increase in variety and polyphonic complexity, throughout the great final act. The mixture of blazing intensity as well as delicacy which Wagner found in Beethoven's *Missa Solemnis*, Fifth, Seventh and Ninth Symphonies, and the late String Quartets (especially the C sharp minor, Opus 131), are reflected in this score. The more intimately we know it, the more do we tend to remember, not so much its initial emotional impact, as the refinement of so many passages, culminating in one of the most exquisite tapestries of interwoven melodies in all music, Isolde's *Liebestod*. Originally, the Prelude was called *Liebestod* (Love -Death), and the final solo, Isolde's *Verklärung* (Transfiguration), which was a much more appropriate description, since its recapitulation of the passionate love duet music of Act Two transfigures it into something calmer, slower, and more truly mystical.

In his essay in the form of a letter, *The Music of the Future* (1860), Wagner considered how, in *Tannhäuser* and *Lohengrin*, the emphasis was increasingly on the 'inner workings of the soul'. When it came to *Tristan*, 'here in perfect confidence, I plunged into the inner depths of soul events, and from the innermost centre of the world, I fearlessly built up its outer form. A glance at the contents of this poem will show you at once that I have rejected the exhaustive detail which an historical poet is obliged to employ so as to clarify the outward developments of his plot, to the detriment of a lucid exposition of its inner motives, and I trusted myself to the latter alone. Life and death, the whole meaning and existence of the outer world, here hang on nothing but the inner movements of the soul. The whole decisive action materializes when the innermost soul demands it, and comes forward to reveal itself with the very shape predicted within the inner shrine'.

Much of his symbolic interpretation of the drama in the light of Schopenhauer and Buddhism, can be read in his fascinating letters to Mathilde Wesendonck and to Liszt (particularly of June 7, 1855). In his programme note for the Prelude, he touched upon musical and poetic elements that apply to the whole work. The musician's problem was 'how to restrain himself, since exhaustion of the theme is quite impossible'. He emphasizes the importance of the theme of Desire [2]:

> In one long breath, he let that unslaked longing swell from the first avowal of the gentlest tremor of attraction, through half-heaved sighs, through hopes and fears, laments and wishes, joy and torment, to the mightiest onset, the most resolute attempt to find the breach, unbarring to the heart a path into the sea of endless love's delight. In vain! Its power spent, the heart sinks back to pine of its Desire—Desire without attainment; for each fruition sows the seeds of fresh Desire, until in its final weariness, the opening eye beholds a glimmer of the highest bliss: it is the bliss of quitting life, of being no more, of last redemption into that wondrous realm from which we stray the furthest when we strive to enter it by fiercest force. Shall we call it Death? Or is it not Night's wonder world, whence—as the story says—an ivy and a vine sprang up in locked embrace over the graves of Tristan and Isolde?

16

A Musical Commentary

Anthony Negus

Act One

Each act of *Tristan and Isolde* has a distinct musical atmosphere. Death hangs over the first act; the second act takes place amidst the scents of a glorious summer night; the bleak sea and burning sun of the third act lead into Tristan's inner suffering. In each there is an elemental climax: the drinking of atonement, the extinguishing of a flaming torch, the final embrace; and the third climax contains the music of both the others. This sequence suggests that the actions of the characters are predestined.

The musical essence of the drama—the love idea—lies in the prelude. Wagner described this as the 'love death' and the end of the opera as 'love's transfiguration'. He repeatedly draws upon it, in its entirety and in fragments. The silences between the phrases are significant; the famous first chord will develop in many directions: here it aspires towards the last phrase [3] which will come to symbolize the workings of fate. Of the themes that follow, the extended cello theme [4] is particularly important. The prelude forms a great arch and begins a recapitulation before one is fully aware of it; the climax, which foreshadows that of Act One, dies away into an ominous cello and double-bass phrase while preparing the way for the young sailor's song.

The elements play a central part in Wagner's work, as *The Ring*'s beginning and end clearly show. Water is particularly important: the sea in *The Flying Dutchman*, the river in *Lohengrin* and the lake in *Parsifal*. In *Tristan* the first act takes place at sea, and in the last act the sea is in view. Moreover the 'sea' motifs in the sailor's song make significant interruptions to the action, for example, at Kurwenal's entrance ('Up! Up! You women!'), when one can almost sense the salt spray, or the cries of 'Loose the anchor!' which precipitate Tristan's decision to drink.

When the curtain rises, Tristan is at the stern of a ship sailing from Ireland to Cornwall, while Isolde is seated motionless on the deck. The song of the Cornish sailors (out of sight) provokes her into telling her story (outlined on page 7) to Brangäne.

The ambiguity, or incompleteness, of the text finds its true explanation in the music. When Isolde sings 'He gazed in my eyes' (solo viola [4]), or 'And his anguish wounded me so', there can be no doubt that she is in love with him, although she is clever at keeping this from others ('the mistress of silence') and even from herself. But she confesses it to herself at *'mir erkoren'* ('destined for

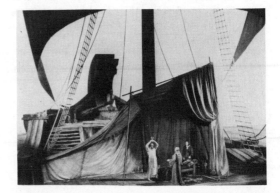

The drink of atonement, at Bayreuth in 1938, designed by Preetorius (Bildarchiv-Bayreuther Festspiele)

me')—the chromatic music of [2]—and sees death as the only solution. Motif [10] (harmonic—like so many in this opera—rather than melodic), which appears for the first time at '*Todgeweihtes Haupt*' ('Death-devoted head'), is one of the musical mainsprings of the work and recurs as many as nine times at key moments in Act One.

It basically contains the chords of A b (woodwind), beside A in a spine-tingling *pianissimo* (brass); a second part suggests C minor; the theme, with two impressive falling octaves, ends with a rhythmic form of the 'fate' phrase representing Isolde's determination to make Tristan drink atonement ([15a] derived from [3]).

In a stormy outburst Isolde calls upon her mother's arts to destroy the ship. The turbulence continues through Brangäne's attempt to soothe her. The phrase at 'Pale and silent/On the voyage;/Food refusing,/Without sleep' will underly Tristan's suffering in Act Three. Though Brangäne sings above it, this music belongs to Isolde; and returns whenever Isolde recalls how she let the sword drop—it suggests that this memory is a traumatic abyss which she must somehow bridge. On the first occasion she describes healing the wound; on the second the orchestra expresses her sense of shame; on the third, when she addresses Tristan, she demands that he atone with the death drink.

Much of this music is lightly accompanied recitative. Brangäne asks Tristan to visit Isolde, and Kurwenal makes an insulting reply culminating in the refrain [12]. The short phrase between these folksong verses expresses the characters' reactions to them: Cosima Wagner's words about *Tristan* spring to mind: the gesture gives rise to the music, not the music to the gesture. As Brangäne returns distraught, the horns [12a] are heard within the orchestral turmoil. The orchestral texture of the music which introduces Isolde's Narration is an essential element of the chromatic descending theme associated with the healing of Tantris [13].

There are two 'periods' (to use Alfred Lorenz's term from *Das Geheimnis der Form bei R. Wagner*) in Isolde's narration, both ending with [12] but, despite the many textual and musical parallels, their characters are different. In the second, Isolde's hurt anger wells up repeatedly [41] as her 'cry from the heart' did in the first. The mood fluctuates between reflection and fury: at the moment of the curse — falling octaves as in the 'death' motif — she must summon all her energies, since the orchestra is required to maintain an uninterrupted *fortissimo* (which is rare for Wagner).

Brangäne points out that Tristan has honoured her by giving up his inheritance of the Cornish crown for her. The music of her consolation has a soothing symmetry. Isolde's passionate discontent is voiced by the orchestra. Brangäne misunderstands her phrase '*Ungeminnt*' ('Unbeloved') which not only indicates again that she loves Tristan but more importantly her belief that he does not love her; the cor anglais theme comes from a less familiar phrase in the prelude [7]. The last part of Brangäne's consolation has a change of metre from 4/4 to 3/4 and the new theme forms an expressive canon, first in the strings and then in the wind, related to the 'love' motif [5] (with its falling seventh) when Brangäne hints at the love potion.

The centre of the act has been reached — and the first phrases of the prelude (without the cello motif) are heard again. By praising the love potion Brangäne unwittingly brings Isolde to the idea of atonement. The ominous *pianissimo* and the bass motif [6] which dominates much of this period suggest the direction of Isolde's thoughts. The selection of the drink, Brangäne's horrified reaction (to the music of the curse), the sailors' calls and Kurwenal's entrance follow thick and fast. It is a relief to hear the 'sea' music as Kurwenal urges the ladies to prepare for landing. Isolde replies, the measured triplets

18

restraining her excitement. She gives the unwilling Brangäne the poison to prepare, quoting her own words back at her ('Have you forgot my mother's arts?') referring now not to the love drink, but to the death drink as the healer of all pain. The 'death' motif reaches for the only time a full resolution on C ('Let death grant her his thanks'). At this still point, the only sound is a quiet roll on the timpani. Kurwenal announces Tristan and the orchestra transforms [10b], the final part of the 'death' motif, into a separate motif. It grows three times out of a unison wind *crescendo*, on each appearance a minor third higher, the third time with trumpets added. In reply, the strings play a treading sarabande rhythm [15b]. This sequence corresponds exactly to the three phrases of the prelude [1]. Tristan's entrance seems anticlimactic — for it was not just his entrance that the music prepared, but the whole course of events to follow. The fate motif [15] dominates the scene up to Tristan's moment of decision, and it is the music of his oath of atonement. As they stand gazing at each other, the poison music in the bass [6] and the string tremolo vividly convey the obsessions of Isolde's mind.

This long scene begins with a duel of words. From Tristan's first speech the tension eases into a formality dominated by [15b] and a more energetic form of [15a] expresses her determination. Tristan's quiet question, 'Cared you for him?', shows that he perceives her true feelings. He offers her his sword to take her revenge but she parries with irony — Mark would hardly be pleased if she was to kill his trustiest knight; instead she demands another atonement and commands Brangäne to prepare the drink. The sailors' cries stir Tristan from a brooding reverie; his words hold the key to the true situation between them: 'The queen of silence / Makes me silent: / For I know what she hides, / What I hide she cannot tell.'

He understands what she remains silent about: that she loves him. He remains silent about what she does not understand: that he loves her. The viola figure [13] and the style of Isolde's cantilena, with extended string writing, recall the third act of *The Valkyrie*. The rhythm of that figure forms the basis of Isolde's scornful outburst when she imagines how Tristan will present her to Mark. As she offers him the cup of poison the full close in C minor is suddenly interrupted by the 'death' harmonies and a string figure that evokes the 'sea' music. Tristan implies that he knows that he is about to drink his death; there is a sense of abandon about the line 'Will cure my hurt completely'. His oath is both tragic and noble. It is prefaced by the most powerful appearance of [15], and an urgent triplet rhythm in the woodwind (which returns when Isolde grasps the cup from him). With Isolde's 'Betrayer! I drink to you!', the music returns to the climax of the prelude and to its opening theme [1].

The effect of the drink is to release the lovers' feelings for each other but not, as Isolde's reproaches in the next act will show, to cancel their previous experience. They both imagine that they are on the threshold of death and that they are about to enter the realm of night, where their love is admissible. Confused and, literally, stupefied, they discover that they are still among the living in the ordinary daylight world. 'Which king?' asks Tristan when Kurwenal points at Mark's approaching boat. Events allow them only a few moments of unconscious rapture; with horror, Isolde learns what Brangäne has done.

Between phrases of the prelude — the shimmering echo of [2] high in the strings is a wonderful new thought — the music graphically depicts their progress from defiance of death (the bass clarinet lays motif [10b] to rest), through their physical reaction to the drink (a sharp-edged passage developed in Act Three) to ardour. Their first words of love — each other's names — are sung to the cello theme [4] which will also be the music of Tristan's death. As Tristan embraces Isolde, the music of the prelude is transformed from languor into energy. Almost immediately the trumpets and chorus announce King Mark's arrival. The lovers exclaim 'yearning enchantment, love overflowing' with a sweep like the waves of the sea — the falling thirds are answered by ascending string phrases [8] and the voices are heard in gradually rising octaves. The duet is interrupted on a long A by the 'sea' music which, transformed, becomes the music of Mark's arrival. Conflicting themes of the two worlds—of night and day — continue to the last bar, where the off-stage trumpets and trombones triumphantly hold the final C major chord of the 'day' motif.

Act Two

A cutting chord of the seventh carries a motif that will be of primary importance in this act [16]. It could be said to represent the pull of the day upon lovers dedicated to the night. Before they can fully lose themselves in their love for one another, Isolde has to express her pent-up reproaches. As they relive the time when Tristan ignored and repressed his love for her, the motif appears in different guises: violent, heroic and poetic. In the quick music it undergoes rapid transformation and in the slow music it binds the whole fabric together.

The act opens with what is, in a sense, an interlude between two long scenes for Tristan and Isolde. The introduction speaks in a new musical language where the string triplets showing Isolde's impatient expectancy, the night sounds ([18] woodwind) and the theme of longing ([2] violins echoed by wind) grow into a welter of chromatic harmony [19]. It avoids a tonal resting place. The music of the climax will return twice in the scene: when Isolde begs Brangäne to extinguish the torch, (the signal for Tristan to come to her), and when she extinguishes it herself. As the offstage hunting horns [20] grow more distant Isolde ceases to believe in their reality and their triplets gradually become a murmuring ripple in the clarinets. The beautiful summer nights that Wagner experienced in Venice perhaps find their tonal expression here.

Brangäne relates (in recitative full of sinister insinuation) her suspicion of Melot. Isolde still believes him to be Tristan's friend and, to Brangäne's clearer warning that the hunt is a trick to betray Tristan, she replies that Melot arranged it to assist them. The music begins here (in D b) with poetic use of the horn calls very gently played by the woodwind — but builds up as Isolde beseeches her companion to extinguish the torch. The passage combines a rhythmic motif exchanged between cellos and violins suggesting Isolde's excitement, with the sustained breadth of her singing line, an invocation to the night. Her *crescendo* of desire is stemmed by Brangäne's emotional effort to make her appreciate the true situation. Although she blames herself for Isolde's terrible plight, Isolde attributes it to Frau Minne, the Goddess of love. Out of the chord [2] on the word '*Zaubers*' grow the chromatic motifs. No better example of the different style of the music in this act could be given than when [10] is woven in at the words 'Life and death she holds in her hand' — the 'death' motif has been transformed into the 'kiss of love'.

Brangäne's almost hysterical third warning begins the musical paragraph which culminates in Tristan's arrival. Isolde's music is more abandoned still (*Immer bewegter*) and reaches a momentous climax at the extinguishing of the torch, which she identifies with the light of day itself [10]. The striding bass phrase represents Tristan's approach. Their embrace is the only *fff* marking

20

in the score, an indication of the extreme care with which Wagner wrote the dynamics. The orchestra is (for him) a small one (no Wagner tubas and only triple woodwind) and his climaxes are conceived over a very large span; although Tristan's arrival is the louder climax, the extinguishing of the torch has a musical significance which will resonate more significantly in the opera.

During the following transition, which has the shortest musical and poetic phrases in *Tristan*, Wagner wrote that the tempo should be motivated by the emotion expressed. For example 'At last! At last! Here on my breast!' should drive on passionately; in 'These thine eyes? This thy mouth?', the tempo should be eased. C major is triumphantly established in a passage of rapture [19c, 21] which includes Isolde's two top Cs. Although the music is overwhelming, it is not all loud: the *fortepiano* markings are notable. The *crescendo* in wind and brass and the hyper-active string figuration give the passage a very full texture which is difficult to control. As quiet passages materialise, Isolde begins their long mutual psycho-analysis. If this is cut one loses not only a very important dimension of the opera but also some of its most fascinating music. The first section, beginning with [16], is Tristan's passionate plaint against the day—fiery with violin semiquaver passages and a quickened form of the motif [16d]. Isolde's [16c] reply is more tender. She blames Tristan for nursing dreams of glory; a reminiscence of [12] here proves melodically indistinguishable from the 'day' motif [16]. The cadences of each section sum up several themes and prepare the subsequent passage. The music often passes into quieter regions in flat keys, notably A*b*, associated with the night.

The dialogue, which has been relatively rapid, is now broken into longer paragraphs. Tristan describes how he set his mind on fame and honour; the vast compound word '*der Welten-Ehren-Tages-Sonne*', is the source of this inspired passage, which settles on a pedal point of A*b* (cello syncopation) anticipating the kernel of the scene to come. The 'day' motif [16] also assumes the poetic qualities it will later have—particularly when played (as here) by the horn. The oboe in E major evokes the radiant image of Isolde which Tristan boasted about. He recalls praising Isolde, his defiance of envy and his determination to sail for Ireland. The climax is [41], the motif that expressed Isolde's fury in the first act—to which the chromatically descending horns add a searing quality. A wealth of contrasting motifs show Isolde's fluctuating emotions of love and reproach. She recalls the intensity of her hatred and her suffering. The only end to this deception seemed to her to be to draw him into death with her; the closeness of love and death is expressed profoundly by the music in Isolde's line 'There we would drink eternal rapture', and in the woodwind writing that transfigures the underlying harmonies of death. Tristan praises the death drink; which, although it deceived him because it was not poison, nevertheless revealed the truth of his love for Isolde to him. The vocal line is particularly important because it anticipates the mood of existence between life and death which he will inhabit after he has been wounded by Melot. Now 'night-sighted', he can appreciate the true glory of Isolde, rather than the empty brilliance of which he had previously talked so much. A stretto-like passage, piling motif upon motif, leads into Isolde's reply that 'the day revenged itself upon him' by giving Isolde to Mark at the moment when Tristan realised his love for her; it is a musical parallel to the final section of Tristan's solo. The shape of the music may best be grasped through listening to the short passacaglia-type bass motif [43] at the line 'And lonely on royal throne', for instance. A simple statement of [16a] sums up the musical panorama, just as the *fortissimo* 'Tristan' chord at Tristan's 'By night enfolded' indicates that the lovers are now fully initiated into the mysteries of the night. The music draws us in to experience this with them. It is fascinating to see how Wagner repeats Tristan's music from *'Was dich umgliss'* ('Around thy head') in a totally different character. There it was brilliant and glamorous; here it is a wisp of flickering night colours. As he sings of 'the day's lies scattered like dust', we sense that we pass through 'the door of the night' [18]; the chromatic harmony of the crucial new motif [22] (related to [10]) is in keeping with the more intricate style of the musical language that has developed. A poetic transition calms the music with just a hint (violas *sforzando*) of the danger in the background. The hardly perceptible rhythmic throb becomes the basis of the whole next section (rhythm [23c]).

' *O sink hernieder Nacht der Liebe* ' ('Oh sink around us/Night of loving') is an invocation to the night to envelop them, and release them from the world. The melody, sung by Tristan, is none other than the notes of the 'Tristan' chord spun into a wonderful legato line [23]; the voices intertwine with each other over two-bar phrases, and with the resolving chords from the song ' *Träume* ' [23b] in the 'Wesendonck Songs'. Isolde's theme ' *Barg im Busen uns sich die Sonne* ' ('In my breast/The sun is declining') [24], which will appear transformed into violent agitation in Act Three, here breathes warmth and peace. Tristan follows with the identical phrase half a tone higher—thereby placing side by side the contrasting tonalities of A♭ and A, the keys of death and of love, just as the two chords were placed side by side in the 'death' motif. The whole of the passage from ' *Barg im Busen* ' proves to be an exact parallel of the first section from ' *O sink Nacht* '. The melody ' *Herz an Herz* ' ('Heart on heart') in B♭ [25] will be developed very fully; in Wagner's sketches it is one of the earliest Tristan melodies.

A voice is heard singing a long-drawn-out melody, ' *Einsam wachend* ' ('Lonely watcher'), like a soul lost in the night. The interweaving lines in the orchestra include ' *Barg im Busen* ' [24] as well as a triplet phrase which will reappear at the cataclysm of Act Three. A tonal centre seems to be reached as the oboe plays [25], where muted horns add a note of warning. This passage has claims to being the most sheerly beautiful piece of sonority in *Tristan*; it certainly caught the imagination of his successors—Schoenberg's *Verklärte Nacht*, the slow movement of Bruckner's 8th Symphony.

Who then was singing? Brangäne on watch warning the lovers that the night cannot last. But we hear her voice through the ears of Tristan and Isolde just as, earlier, we heard the horns through Isolde's ears. It is as though we hear the warning sounds of the outer world through veils of quiet rapture.

The scale of this love scene may be realised in that Brangäne's second warning leads to an animated development of [25] a semitone higher, when the roles of the lovers are reversed. The text becomes a philosophical discussion, couched in tender expressions of love, about day and death, about the nature of their love, and about the very word 'and' that binds their names together. The new paragraph begins with Tristan's '*Unsre Liebe?*' ('Our loving?') in which common time takes over from triple time. The violins' link to Isolde's reply is memorable for its stillness, and the following passage for three clarinets (including bass) over a horn pedal must have fascinated Alban Berg.

One of the great qualities of Wagner's invention is that the listener senses something new has been reached here. For those hearing *Tristan* for the first time, but who know Isolde's final lament, the passage 'So let us die' ('*So stürben wir*') [26] will seem familiar; it is identical. Almost imperceptibly the music glides into the last phrase of Brangäne's warning. It is as though we were unconscious during the earlier part of her song and only gradually became aware of it.

The lovers launch into an intense duet, a true love death, a *Liebestod*. The motif '*O ew'ge Nacht*' is that motif of longing for night that has played such a fundamental role, [22]; the '*Träume*' chords [23b] are also prominent. The music of the death song (now in B major) returns in a very different character: originally solemn, it is here rhapsodic. The four-note turn—the very symbol of romantic music which Wagner so ennobled—and the descending phrase which it launches [27], appear in the vocal line and in the woodwind; as the text speaks of 'boundless realms of rapture', the music seems to create wider and wider spaces of ecstasy. The lovers abandon themselves with phrases that build up to a climactic surge. The *molto crescendo* after a sudden *piano* is cruelly interrupted by the harshest discord in *Tristan* and Brangäne's scream. The outer world has encroached.

With trumpets and trombones added to the horns, the music of the hunt sounds garish. Melot's phrase, punctuated by two stabbing figures in the violas, recalls that this catastrophe was foreshadowed.

King Mark cannot comprehend how Tristan could betray him. His first phrase conveys his contempt for Melot's belief that his honour has been saved. The opening section of his long solo is at once a tribute to Tristan's former love and a deep reproach. A plaintive descending figure in the bass clarinet [28] breaks his phrases. A new theme [29] becomes the leading motif, accompanied primarily by lower strings. His touching reference to a dead, childless wife, explains his love for Tristan as a son.*

The middle section—marked much slower—is his tribute to Isolde, and his sense that she was untouchable. His phrases are *legato* arches, at first with the cellos, then with the first violins; a passage of very quiet declamation conveys his most private thoughts, the very secrets of his bedchamber.

In the third section King Mark angrily reflects that the cruellest wound that Tristan has inflicted is the loss of his honour. The cellos and bass clarinet have been playing an agitated rising phrase; and he expresses his despair in the same music as Isolde in Act One [41]. His vocal phrase for the lines, 'What no heaven can heal,/Why this hell must I suffer?', is very closely related to Wotan's outburst in Act Two of *The Valkyrie*—both characters have been caught in a web of their own making. He asks the unanswerable question—who shall explain how the true came to be false? The question calls up the essence of the *Tristan* music—its very opening; the resolutions of the first two phrases go a step further than before, as Tristan says that he can neither tell him the answer, nor could Mark conceive it.

In a solemn strophe Tristan offers to lead Isolde to the land of oblivion, the land from which his mother (dying in childbirth) sent him. It is the land into which he plunges when he falls upon Melot's sword. The music of this verse evokes a sense of the primal mystery of nature [30], and is not far removed from the annunciation of death to Siegmund by Brünnhilde (*The Valkyrie* Act Two). Isolde's reply, to almost the same music, contains a gentle smiling reproof: since she followed him when he was faithless to her, it is hardly necessary to ask now whether she would accompany him, wherever he may lead. The languorous music of their love provokes Melot into violent action. 'Can you bear the disgrace?', he asks Mark. Tristan's nobility is illustrated by

---

*Tristan, according to Gottfried, was Mark's nephew. His peculiar status as the man to whom Mark owed his kingdom (after he slew Morold) and his bride (when he won Isolde) suggests an Oedipus complex relationship.

23

the way he excuses Melot's treachery by supposing he was, as any man would be, unable to resist Isolde's beauty, and that he only acted out of jealousy. Tristan's attack on Melot is the natural reaction of a knight whose honour is challenged. He drops his guard in the sudden realisation that death alone will release him from life without honour. Isolde, in Act One, also saw death as a solution to the intolerable prospect of a life of shame. But, just as Tristan then found himself alive after he had drunk what he accepted as poison, so he now finds himself still living after Melot's attack. With this new wound he enters the world between life and death. The 'King Mark' theme resounds tragically in the trumpets and more compassionately in the horns; the curtain falls to a powerful D minor chord.

Act Three

One of the wonders about the third act of *Tristan* is its form; even without a thorough knowledge of it, one may sense its symphonic nature—above all in Tristan's monologue. If the first act belongs to Isolde, then the last is fundamentally Tristan's. We experience with Tristan the pain he feels, deprived of his beloved, his great longing for death to unite them both, and the agony of returning to consciousness, with all the renewed pain and longing which that involves. The 'old sad melody' (the ' *alte traurige Weise*'), heard at the outset, returns to evoke his earliest memories of his parents' deaths. The past and present constantly intermingle: the wound he received from Melot is confused with the one which Isolde healed. Like Isolde's Narration, Tristan's monologue ends in a curse—on the love drink and himself. His blissful vision of Isolde and Kurwenal's loving concern form the slow movement of the symphony, while the ship's arrival is its *scherzo*; its *finale* stretches from the death of Tristan through the arrival of the second ship to Isolde's transfiguration.

The introduction is not so much an entity in itself, like the opening prelude, but a part of the first scene. The first chord sets a tone of foreboding that is sustained through the desolation of the rising thirds in the violins to the sadness of the new theme in horns and cellos [33]. The theme [31] that grows out of the opening chord is a diatonic version of [2].

Like the young sailor's song, the shepherd's song [34] is a mixture of the sophisticated and the natural. Different episodes are developed during the course of the act, the most significant being its opening fifth, a direct inversion of the 'day' motif. The shepherd and Kurwenal are evidently long-standing friends. The evocation of emptiness at 'öd und leer das Meer' has become famous through T.S. Eliot's *The Waste Land*.

The hardly perceptible entrance of the cellos and double-basses beneath the melody and Tristan's first words mark his very gradual return to consciousness. Kurwenal's reaction is incredulous, then overjoyed at these signs of life. Sweeping violin phrases reminiscent of the end of *Siegfried* Act Two settle into a more formal passage [35] when Kurwenal explains that he is in Kareol. The diatonic style of the music anticipates *The Mastersingers*; it has the firmness and uncomplicated directness of Kurwenal's devotion to Tristan. Harmonically distant chords suggest Tristan's painful efforts to become aware of where he is. They evoke something of Tannhäuser's return from Rome.

As Tristan struggles to speak, the music takes up again what was so faintly begun when he awoke. The descending bass line leads to the quietest of reminiscences of [23]. Total oblivion (' *Urvergessen*') is one of the stillest moments: while Tristan longs for release, life courses back into him. The theme of longing [2] introduces a large scale passage whose climax is Tristan's curse upon the day—'Must you ever watch my pain?'. The self-torturing quality of Tristan's agony is expressed in music not heard since Brangäne's description of Isolde as 'pale and silent' in Act One. The motif of death [10] and the rhythms associated with Tristan's fight with Melot reappear as Tristan describes the door of death closing behind him; a restless treatment of [25] accompanies his return to consciousness, with little accented stabs of pain. After the climax on the word 'Ewig', Tristan relives the seemingly endless moments in the summer night as he waited for Isolde to extinguish the torch.

It may now be observed how Wagner uses the separate phrases of [2] to form bridges between sections. Phrase (a) introduces Kurwenal's lively response. Tristan's mind is, however, far away (a faint tremolo of strings). It is then that, with phrase (b), Kurwenal describes why he sent for Isolde. We hear again the rhythmic figure of his joy [45], the music of the wound [13], and that of Isolde's love [21]. The music of the lovers' embrace in Act Two [36] eases in momentum as Tristan says to Kurwenal, 'You hated the one I hated, and loved the one I loved'. It foreshadows Eva's tribute to Sachs in Act Three of The Mastersingers and there is a clear psychological parallel. The climax of Tristan's delusion that Isolde's ship has been sighted evokes Act Two [23b], and his relapse is correspondingly great when the shepherd's pipe indicates that the sea is still empty. The melody [34], beginning at (d), is spun out almost into timelessness to a quiet string tremolo, the woodwind taking up phrases where the offstage cor anglais leaves off. Tristan reflects upon the deaths of his father who begat him and died, and his mother who died giving birth to him. The moment is as fundamental as Siegfried's reflections upon his mother, the psychological explanation for a theme in the Tristan saga that Wagner did not otherwise pursue: Tristan born to sadness. It is a moment of pause, the muted strings hushed and intimate. The oboe and clarinet take up the melody alternately as he questions why he was born. His answer, ''Tis yearning and dying', is the pivot that releases the next musical section. It seems to him that it is this intolerable longing which prevents him from dying.

The arresting orchestral chord, as imposing as the first chord of Act Two, brings two motifs [16, 34a] together for the first time. In the strength of the music can be felt the progress that Tristan has made in his voyage of self-discovery.

Theme [13] has been introduced almost imperceptibly. Wagner expressed delight at the way it combined with [34a] in a letter to Mathilde Wesendonck. There is a short glimpse of happiness as the orchestra describes the wind gently blowing Tristan's ship to 'Ireland's child'; within four bars, four tunes combine so naturally that one is hardly aware of it: [34] (a) and (b), [16] and [13] for the only time in the major key.

Tristan's delirium may best be described in four sections: (i) Isolde tore open the wound she had healed but then let the sword fall*; she gave him the drink in which he hoped to find total relief; instead he is unable to die. (ii) The drink races to his brain; nowhere can he find peace, for the night casts him relentlessly into the day. (iii) The effect of the excoriating sun on his brain, the very height of Tristan's delirium, is textually not far from Amfortas's suffering (Parsifal). (iv) Guilt. He himself brewed the poison from the sad plight of his parents, tears of love from time immemorial, laughter and crying, bliss and pain. He curses the drink and himself for brewing it.

---

* 'But with the sword she struck again'. This line is ambiguous. Tristan perhaps means that Isolde threatened to strike him with Morold's sword, which had once wounded him.

25

Like the text, the music glides from one thought into the next in a process of continuous development. (i) It returns to [13]. The poison motif in the bass anticipates the text. The crux of the music and text follows, and for the only time Tristan sings [1], the cello theme heard at the opening of the prelude.in this polyphony [2a] and [26] are joined by the now-omnipresent [34a]. (ii) The music of the atonement drink is extended by the violins and violas with cruelly difficult phrases. (iii) A repetition of the music that led up to Tristan's curse on the day. Perhaps the most amazing passage of all has phrase (c) from the 'alte Weise' in the bass, constant triplets in the wind, the motif of longing (horn and oboe) and phrase (a) of the 'alte Weise' (violin and piccolo). It intensifies with the description of pain and finds a tragic release in the line 'Dark fatal drink!' (iv) A new motif [37] which recurs ten times contains inverted elements of the music already associated with suffering and longing. It begins with the emotionally powerful effect of two beats which swell from *piano* to *fortissimo* whilst the harmony changes underneath. In addition, [2] in the brass leads to the most shattering of the four climaxes within this paragraph: (i) chord of A minor, 'the drink'; (ii) Db 'eternal suffering'; (iii) E minor, again 'the drink', (iv) F# minor, the curse. Although the climax is an F# minor chord, the second and less violent curse—'And curse him by whom 'twas brewed!'—brings it back to F minor. This concludes the 'first movement' of the 'symphony'.

Seven times the new motif [36] tumbles violently through the orchestra. As Tristan had paid tribute to him, so now Kurwenal does to Tristan. The quality of Kurwenal's love is like Wotan's for Brünnhilde, or Siegmund's for the exhausted Sieglinde in the second act of The Valkyrie [47]. Out of the gentle throbbing of the clarinets and horn on the 'Tristan' chord which suggests Tristan's heart-beat, the oboe begins a new passage with the motif of longing [2]. Tristan's first words as he revives are, 'The ship?', so that he returns psychologically to the point at which he collapsed the first time. Oboe, clarinet and solo violin depict a calm and beautiful image of Isolde. The horns' gentle [25] leads to a *cantabile* recollection of [38].

Tristan urges Kurwenal to watch for the ship. Wagner's genius for transition is here at its height—within this very short space he leads from despair into the exhilaration of the shepherd's happy tune [39] when Isolde's ship is sighted. The musical foundation of this 'scherzo' is [24] in the bass, which is literally turned upside down when Tristan loses sight of the ship and imagines that even Kurwenal has betrayed him. The chords which punctuate Kurwenal's exit to fetch Isolde are of a similar character to Siegfried's departure into the woods (Siegfried Act One).

Tristan is left completely alone; his excitement is expressed by constant changes of metre—unusually for Wagner—and by the syncopated striving effect of the familiar [24]. More themes from the past return, and Tristan's almost demented jubilation is expressed in 5/4 time. It is the beginning of another parallel: through fragments of [38] ('Ach Isolde') Tristan sings of fighting with his wound bleeding. At the lines 'She who can close/My wound forever', the music reaches its climax with the 5/4 music now played *fortissimo*, punctuated by the triplets of the trumpets and timpani, as Tristan tears off his bandages. And from this climax comes a heightened and shortened repetition as the fever increases and draws us back yet again to the moment *before* Isolde extinguished the torch in Act Two. Now he hears her: 'What, I hear the light? / The torch-light, ah! / The torch now is out. / To her! To her!'

Tristan's words, wild and paradoxial as they are, are the key to the opera. Isolde is 'the light': although he cannot see her, he can hear her voice. He imagines that he sees again the sign—the extinguishing of the torch-light—for him to run to her. The trumpets sound the 'death' theme [10] and, in an extraordinary polyphony, theme [24] and Brangäne's watch song may be heard. The opening phrase of the prelude then recurs, as it did when Isolde took the death drink from Tristan. It fades away to a seemingly timeless suspension on [36]. The cellos resume the 'Tristan' theme [4] for the last time. Thus this climax combines those of both previous acts. Isolde tells Tristan that she has come faithfully to die with him. The section expands into grief with a new motif [40]. The sadness of her separateness finds expression in [33] (woodwind), then strings [22] with [40]. Much of the death song music [26] returns, anticipating her Transfiguration. For the last time she reproaches Tristan but he cannot now even hear her grief. The motif [40], formerly a quiet symbol of the mystery of death, is now climactic. The music comes full cycle to a repeated E♭, which anticipates the final D# between the final bars of the opera. On the dominant chord of D, a key which for Wagner implies transcendence, Isolde imagines that he awakes. In mood and key the music could move straight into the Transfiguration; that it does not is an example of Wagner's art of preparing the mood and then delaying its fulfilment.

The next scene is something of a shock, for there is more activity in five minutes than in the whole act. The shepherd announces a second ship and Kurwenal goes to muster a defence force. The steersman of Isolde's ship rushes in to sing four bars: that they are overpowered by the superior force of Mark and Melot. Brangäne and Melot are heard offstage; Kurwenal is aroused into wild action. He kills Melot and attacks the others with renewed vigour. Mark is heard offstage; Brangäne rushes to Isolde, Mark enters and Kurwenal, mortally wounded, struggles to die near Tristan. The music is appropriately energetic, deriving from [36] and [34d]. When Brangäne and Mark enter, the orchestra overwhelms everything with the climax of Isolde's mourning. Kurwenal's death is a touching summary of his faithful love for the master whose closest companion he was.

It has humorously been observed that Mark and Brangäne are left to bury the dead. Mark gives way to grief. Brangäne tells Isolde that she has told Mark the story of the love drink and that he had come to give her to Tristan. Recalling Brangäne's consolatory music in Act One Mark again asks: 'Why this to me?' He has been told what happened; but he cannot understand it. The hushed opening phrase of the death song [26] has sounded between these sections, each time a semitone higher: first, at Isolde's revival (in F); at the end of Brangäne's section, in G♭; and after Mark's last phrase, in G. The way has thus been prepared for the actual opening in A♭ of Isolde's Transfiguration.

Although the music (from the bass clarinet solo) is a repetition of the second act music in slower form, the new vocal line creates the impression of a new composition. When Isolde asks a series of increasingly rhetorical questions, her words are inextricably bound up with the music and are themselves music; one is reminded of the line in *The Magic Flute*: '*Durch des Tones Macht*'— 'through the power of music'; or of the Schlegel verse that prefaces Schumann's *Fantasy in C*:

Pervading all the notes that sound	Durch alle Töne tönet
Through this multi-coloured earthly dream	Im bunten Erdentraum
Is a single soft sustained tone	Ein leiser Ton gezogen
To be heard by the quiet and secret listener.	Für dem der heimlich lauscht.

The gentleness evoked here by singer and orchestra is 'all revealing'. Only just before the climax—interrupted in the second act, here accomplished—do the words become a statement.

In the welcoming wave,	I'm drowning,
Holding all.	Unaware,
I'm sinking,	Highest love!

The word '*Welt*' has already been the source of important climaxes in Act Two ('*Welterlösend aus*' and '*Selbst dann bin ich die Welt*'); this marks the consummation of the 'day' motif. The long winding-down of the final bars matches the long circling build-up that has preceded them. The motif of longing [2] comes to rest; the sad tone of the cor anglais, formerly so all-pervading, is significantly absent from the three final B major chords. This key of B which now resolves the scenes between Tristan and Isolde is yet not the key of the whole work, but its dominant. E major is the key of the love idea, of the unachievable, experienced at length only in Tristan's vision of Isolde. The climax of the Transfiguration has veered between chords of these two keys in such a way as to leave not a little ambiguity as to which should carry the greater weight; it is one of the profound joys in the experience of *Tristan* that such questions may never be finally resolved.

Richard Wagner in 1863, photographed by Mebius in Moscow.

The Wesendonck villa at Zurich, with 'Asyl' the cottage built for Wagner.

The Staging of 'Tristan and Isolde':
Landmarks along the Appian way

Patrick Carnegy

It is with an immense feeling of relief that one turns from the infinitely awkward problem of staging *The Ring* to that of staging *Tristan* — a single opera, and one which, if no less inspired by myth, is at least free from any obligation to dwarfs and giants, to horses, bears and ravens, to underwater spectaculars and fire-girt mountain peaks.

There is a powerful line of argument that a concert performance of *Tristan*, preferably heard with one's back to the singers and orchestra, is the ideal performance, and that any stage representation is a sin against the essential nature of the work. For, of all Wagner's dramas, *Tristan* is the most sheerly musical, the most perfect expression of Schopenhauer's assertion of the supremacy of music over all other arts. As Paul Bekker once observed, 'Upon the stage walk sounds, not people'.

The opera is, after all, concerned with the invisible, interior lives of Tristan and Isolde, lives which had found no entirely satisfactory expression in literature until Wagner claimed them for music. For Wagner, feeling enshrined in music is the whole truth; everything else, all action, even that between Tristan and Isolde, is error and delusion. The ruling tension is between the rival realms of darkness and light. This polarity is symbolic in the widest sense; the entire opera is a hymn to the Night, although even here Tristan and Isolde fail to find erotic fulfilment and must seek their Nirvana in a mystic union beyond death.

The opposition of the values of Night and Day offers a glimmer of stage potential, of a theatrical possibility which, while not compromising the rule of Night, would allow *something* to be shown as well as heard. For if the drama tells of a contest between Night and Day, then light there has to be, even if only to intensify the eventual triumph of darkness. In this respect one can regard *Tristan* as the Romantic antithesis of *The Magic Flute*, where the Apollonian Sarastro vanquishes the Queen of the Night. Both operas enshrine symbolic confrontations between reason and instinct, between light and darkness; and if they arrive at diametrically opposite conclusions, this underlines the enormous shift in sensibility between 1791 and 1857, the year in which Wagner began the prose sketch of *Tristan*. That shift was apparent only in the concept of *Tristan*, and not at all in what it really looked like at its first stage performance in King Ludwig II's court theatre on June 10,1865. The general mode of staging, which relied on the steady illumination of painted sets — complete with all appropriate shadows and highlights — was not significantly different from what one would have seen in Schikaneder's original production of *The Magic Flute*.

It is an immensely puzzling paradox that the stagings Wagner was able to secure for his revolutionary dramas were so conservative, so limited to the conventional visual taste of his time. As his grandson Wieland said, 'It is an insult to Wagner the composer to identify his mythological conceptions with the notorious mediocrity of nineteenth-century impotent and pseudo-naturalistic painters, who sought without making any original contribution to the process to adapt the achievements of classicism and romanticism to the taste of the *nouveau riche*'. Of course Ludwig's Hoftheater at Munich aimed very much higher than that; but the mid nineteenth-century stage had but one

Actual 19th century staging rarely lived up to the designer's vision.
Above: sketch by Max and Gotthold Brückner for Act I when the
opera was first performed at Bayreuth in 1886.
Below: photograph of the setting itself. The Brückner brothers ran
a studio which designed all kinds of productions for leading
theatres.

Below: Adolphe Appia's design for Kareol in the 1923 La Scala
production conducted by Toscanini. The floor drops from the
platforms at stage-right representing the wall; beyond these only
the sky could be seen – the sea across which Isolde is hurrying to
Tristan had to be imagined lying 'öd und leer' far below.

ambition, namely to emulate the scenic marvels achieved at the Paris Opéra for the grandiose works of Scribe and Meyerbeer. Even as Wagner hated everything about this kind of 'culinary' theatre, to the point that his own reforms were conceived in direct opposition to it, he nevertheless had to make the best of its visual language for the Munich premières of *Tristan* and *The Mastersingers*, of *Rhinegold* and *Valkyrie*.

Although Wagner's dissatisfaction with this high court style was to lead directly to the neo-Greek enterprise of Bayreuth, even there his energies were directed towards refining contemporary stage practice rather than inventing a new one as wholly original as his musical conceptions. The scenic wonders which Wagner demanded for *The Ring* were nothing if not an attempt to outdo Meyerbeer. Wagner's stage reforms were carried out within that overall ambition. They had largely to do with the *means* of theatrical presentation, not its end. And those means were not chiefly concerned with scenery and lighting, but with the singer, whom Wagner taught to act with total commitment to the drama.

So when Wagner expressed his enthusiasm for the Munich *Tristan*, what he really meant was that he had found in Ludwig Schnorr von Carolsfeld and his wife Malvina an exceptional understanding of his musico-dramatic rhetoric, the very thing which he knew was essential to the success of the piece.

Ludwig's court-painters could be counted on to furnish agreeable decor in the accepted vein of Romantic naturalism, and Wagner hardly troubled to comment on it. What did stir him was the Schnorrs' uncanny understanding and their eloquent delivery of vocal lines which were then totally incomprehensible to most singers — hence the the abortive attempts to secure earlier premières for *Tristan* at Karlsruhe and Vienna. The intensity of Ludwig Schnorr's performance moved Wagner so profoundly that he reiterated his old fear that only mediocre performances could save him, for good ones would surely drive people mad.(Within six weeks of the *Tristan* première, Schnorr was dead from typhus, the fever having apparently been excited by a chill caused by an icy draught from the wings as he had lain sweating from the supreme exertions demanded by the third act. Schnorr's colleagues unkindly attributed his death to the effects of the opera itself.)

Tristan was not staged at Bayreuth until 1886, three years after Wagner's death. During his lifetime performances that he regarded as competent were given elsewhere, most notably in Berlin in 1876 (nine in all). It is remarkable that witnesses of those early performances have so very little to say about the stagings, which were praised by those who hated the music as highly as by those who were impressed by it. The settings were the one contribution which could be taken for granted; it was everything else that was startling, most particularly the music and the fact that so very little actually happened on stage.

It is, however, to one altogether exceptional witness of Wagner's own stagecraft that we owe the revolution in practice and in attitude that has occurred since then. In its shift from representational scenery to an essentially abstract style, this revolution offers remarkable parallels with that in the visual arts which has led, via symbolism, expressionism and cubism, to every variety of non-representational experiment. Many of the artists concerned — Kandinsky, Picasso, Kokoschka, Alfred Roller, Oskar Schlemmer, Moholy-Nagy — were also active in the theatre. But the single most important innovator was a Swiss musician and artist who, although he dedicated his entire life to the theatre, and to Wagner in particular, met with general

31

incomprehension. The detailed scenarios prepared by Adolphe Appia (1862-1928) mostly remained as blueprints and, with one notable exception, reached stage performance in his lifetime only in private salons or esoteric theatres (notably that of Emil Jacques-Dalcroze, inventor of Eurythmics). Appia was 19, a shy music student from Geneva, when he first visited Bayreuth in 1882 for the première of *Parsifal*. He was overwhelmed by the music but deeply upset by Paul Joukovsky's decorative, quasi-realistic settings which Appia felt to be in conflict with the spiritual quality of the music. The essence of his critique was that while Wagner's music embodied a drama that was always developing, and rich in every graduation of light and shade, the Bayreuth scenic conception was too static and inflexible. When night fell on Brünnhilde's rock and the flames flared up, or when she awoke to greet the sun, the lighting — still gas, one must remember — allowed of effects little better than it being turned up or down. Appia especially hated footlights — the epitome of unnatural lighting. The sun, he remarked, was not generally observed to do its work from below. His conclusion was blunt: 'one can assert without exaggeration that no one has yet *seen* a Wagnerian drama on the stage'.

Appia believed that the only reliable guide as to what ought to be seen on the stage is the music. Just as music is quintessentially dynamic, so must the stage-picture be. Nothing could be more static than scenery painted on flats, and therefore this must be abolished. Stage settings should be suggestive, or even altogether abstract, in order that they might be timeless in themselves, hence capable of seeming to change with time even as the music does.

This seems impossible until one remembers the potential of stage lighting. Appia saw that the future of scenic design would be determined by the electric lighting console, orchestrating the play of light upon the stage in exact sympathy with the music. He believed that there was a powerful affinity between music and light, in that both expressed what Schopenhauer called 'the inner essence of phenomena'. And light could also imitate phenomena (i.e. be realistic in the evocation of fire, clouds, water, etc.) just as music could. Appia believed that sets should be of solid construction, using ramps and flights of steps. Costumes and make-up were to be equally simple, acquiring expressive vitality from the lighting and the movements of the singers. Music, which exists in time, must also define the stage space, thus fulfilling Gurnemanz's observation to Parsifal as the forest begins to transform itself into the Hall of the Grail: '*Du siehst, mein Sohn, zum Raum wird hier die Zeit*' — here time becomes space. The text of *Tristan* is rich in metaphysical doubt about the reliability of all sense data, as in Tristan's great cry, '*Wie hör ich das Licht?*' ('Do I hear the light?') — expressing a feeling to which Baudelaire, poet of '*Correspondances*' would have been profoundly sympathetic.

The goal was to clear the stage for the singing actor. Everything visual was to be focused on him. Just as the space around him was to be determined by the music, so were his movements (with the help of eurythmic training), gestures and vocal expression.

What Appia wanted above all was to interiorize Wagner's works, and nothing suited this aim better that *Tristan*, which Toscanini called him out of obscurity to design for La Scala in 1923 (Appia had in fact made his first designs for *Tristan* in the 1890s). He began by designing the second act. He explained that by starting with that act which required the severest 'scenic reduction' he would be committed to no more than the barest necessities for the third and first acts.

The underlying purpose was to help 'the audience see the drama through

Above: Act I at Bayreuth in 1952. Wagner's grandson Wieland reduced the staging to the structural essentials of the composer's own conception. The enormous tent divided the ship into two areas — downstage for Isolde, and upstage (when the drapes opened), the domain of Tristan.

Act III in Wolfgang Wagner's production of 1957. In its exploitation of light and shadow, and of solid shapes, this was closer to Appia than the severe abstraction of Wieland Wagner's metaphysical approach.

Below: Act III of Wieland Wagner's 1952 staging. The tree and every suggestion of a castle courtyard have been taken away, leaving Tristan and Kurwenal on a purgatorial promontory at the frontiers of existence.

the eyes of the hero and heroine'. For Act One there was an enormous tent, or rather very long, dark-reddish drapes dividing the ship into two areas. In Appia's words, 'The ship [was] simple, expressive, very close, without mast, some ropes, very large helm'. According to his biographer, Walther Volbach, 'While the tent remained closed it was starkly illuminated so that the characters were entirely visible. When the curtain opened, much of this light was dimmed to make the tent appear in silhouette'.

For Toscanini and the singers the six performances were a huge success, but the staging met with general hostility. One favourable voice described it as 'a very beautiful experiment', hoping that the distinctly cool reception would deter neither Appia, nor Gordon Craig, from continuing their fight for scenic reform. Toscanini himself was disheartened by the production's failure to win over more than a handful of connoisseurs, and *Tristan* was never given again at La Scala in the remaining years of his directorship.

Although Appia is certainly the pivotal figure in the history of *Tristan* staging, many others found Wagner's instructions unsatisfactory. At the Vienna Opera in 1903 Mahler and Alfred Roller, then president of the Secession artists' association, produced a *Tristan* in whose second act, according to Josef Gregor, 'the play of light of the torch and the deep blue night were as unforgettable as the pale sulphurous rays which suffused the horizon after Melot's betrayal'.

Meyerhold staged the opera in 1909 in St Petersburg. He wrote a fine essay on *Tristan* which shows that his ideas are greatly indebted to Appia. Stage practice, however, still lagged behind theory. As Edward Braun tells us, while Meyerhold's 'plastic groupings against relief settings, and the measured, eloquent movements of the characters, were a revelation to an operatic public inured to flat stages and stock gestures', the settings and costumes were less successful. Their inspiration went right back to Gottfried von Strassburg's epic Tristan poem and the result was 'a series of settings and costumes based on 13th-century miniatures which hovered uneasily between representation and stylization'.

Siegfried Wagner, who took over the Bayreuth Festival in 1908, had no more time for radical stage reform than his mother Cosima. He went to some pains to disassociate himself publicly from the Appian way. Nevertheless, when Siegfried eventually brought *Tristan* back to the Festspielhaus in 1927 it was at least in a fully 3-dimensional staging. (In 1930, the year of Siegfried's death, this production was conducted by Toscanini.)

It was not until the postwar Bayreuth of Wieland and Wolfgang Wagner that the seeds sown by Appia came to fruition. That the apotheosis of his work should have been at Bayreuth — the perpetual goal of his ambitions — seems only just, and an ironic revenge on the citadel which had so scornfully repulsed him in his own lifetime. When the Festival reopened in 1951 the Wagner grandsons were naturally eager to disassociate themselves from Hitler's attempt to turn Bayreuth into a temple of the Thousand-Year Reich, and they were also seriously short of cash. But it would be wrong to dismiss their espousal of Appian simplicity as prompted by no more than political prudence, or economic necessity. Bayreuth's reforms of the 1950s and 60s were at least half a century overdue. Appia's programme was a tremendous gift to Wieland and Wolfgang Wagner. But they were very much more than stage technicians working to another man's blueprint. They proved themselves stage artists in their own right (see accompanying illustrations and captions) by transforming Appia's ideas into a language for evoking the symbolic and archetypal content in Wagner's works.

Wieland Wagner's treatment of the crucial moment after the drinking of the love potion was characteristic of the hard questions he was forever asking of the dramatic motivation. There was no long pause while the potion takes effect and Tristan and Isolde gradually become aware of their feelings. Instead, they rushed immediately into each other's arms. For, as Wieland, like Thomas Mann before him, was well aware, the love potion might just as well have been pure water. It is enough that the lovers *believe* they have drunk their death, and then naturally rush to spend their last moments in each other's arms. After all, Wagner's own dramatic instinct had rejected earlier versions of the legend, where the love potion was the mainspring of the story. The point of Wagner's conception is that Tristan and Isolde are in love from the very first moment when they looked into each other's eyes — and that happened long before the beginning of the opera.

In Wieland's 1958 Stuttgart production (Act I, above left) the tent fabric falls in a catenary, while the sides of the boat are swept up and back into a vanishing prow. This, one might say, pointed forward to Wieland's last and greatest production (above right), first seen at Bayreuth in 1962. The prow detached itself completely and towered over the action, being all that was left to remind one of the ship and its rudder. The other two acts were also dominated by phallic images: a Barbara Hepworth-like giant bodkin for the second act, and for the third a sharp, pierced segment of rock presided over Tristan's delirium. The lighting was cold, eerie greens and airless grey-blues.

Looking to the future, now that the symbolic and mythological dimension of *Tristan* has been so brilliantly explored, it may be time again to reinvoke specific times and places, to ask of *Tristan* — though certainly with less intrinsic justification — the kind of questions which Patrice Chéreau asked of *The Ring* in his Bayreuth centenary production. 'As a man of the theatre', says Chéreau, 'I find it impossible to have costumes and scenery without relating them specifically to a particular time.' In the case of the 1976 Bayreuth *Ring* this meant casting Wotan and family as the aristocracy of 1848, with Bakunin and Co. piling logs around them, while down on the dam on the Rhine, its daughters toted for custom in a froth of scarlet petticoat.

The last word can be left with Wagner. Finding himself tied in a Gordian knot by efforts to fulfil the letter of his stage directions, he triumphantly observed that these directions 'must remain puzzles for aesthetic criticism,... hints for acting, stimuli for the creative imagination'.

An Introduction to the German Text

Martin Swales and Timothy McFarland

Wagner is different from so many of the great opera composers in that he did not draw on the services of a Da Ponte, a Boito, or a Hofmannsthal. The text, like the music, was of his own making. He once wrote: 'I can conceive a subject only when it comes to me in such a form that I myself cannot distinguish between the contribution of the poet and that of the musician'. For the subject-matter of his dramatic works he constantly turned to the legacy of the German Middle Ages, understood in the nineteenth century, somewhat broadly, as embracing the Norse *Vǫlsunga Saga* and lays of the *Edda*, and chivalric romances such as *Tristan* and *Parzival* which were heavily indebted to French models. He perceived and refashioned this material, of course, through a sensibility that reflected the artistic and cultural concerns of his own age and society. The Romantic generation had seen the Middle Ages as a period of profound mythological and philosophical significance. Novalis, perhaps the greatest of the German Romantic poets, wrote a famous essay in celebration of the Christian Middle Ages. He also wrote a series of short, ecstatic poems in prose and verse, the *Hymns to Night* (1799), in which his longing for union with his beloved beyond the grave gives rise to an erotic and mystical celebration of Night as the realm of the highest experience and truth. The impulses derived from Romantic medievalism and from Novalis's *Hymns* can be felt clearly in Wagner's *Tristan*.

Moreover, in the 1850's when he was working on *Tristan*, Wagner was profoundly influenced by his reading of Schopenhauer. He was drawn to the philosopher's sombre doctrine of the world as Will, as the orgiastic tumult and flux of rampant life. Here, for Schopenhauer, is the tragic ground of the human drama: man is 'individuated', a tiny cork of selfhood buffeted by the elemental energies of the Will. In order to escape the suffering entailed in these buffetings, man seeks release from individuation—either in a return to the primal matter of the Will, or in an escape from the Will's clutches. In Wagner's *Tristan*, the lovers seek both: submersion and transcendence. Moreover, for Schopenhauer music expressed the very groundswell of the Will itself. Listening to Wagner's score, one has some idea of what Schopenhauer meant: against the ceaseless current of the orchestral writing the human voice and its medium—language—function as the individuated part of this extraordinary symphonic texture.

In Gottfried von Strassburg's early thirteenth-century courtly romance *Tristan*, Wagner found the correlative for his Romantic and Schopenhauerian world-view, and it is noteworthy that his *Tristan* text is much more faithful to its source than is the case with either *The Ring* or *Parsifal*. Wagner perceived the power of Gottfried's story as residing in a passion that not only undermines the values of feudal loyalty and honour, subverting the institutions of marriage and kingship, but which also strikes at the roots of individuation itself. Gottfried's poem tells us about

A man, a woman; a woman, a man:
Tristan, Isolde; Isolde, Tristan

and celebrates the suffering and death they accept for love in a highly sophisticated rhetorical language which is not afraid to invoke the most sublime religious parallels: 'Their life, their death are our bread. Thus lives their life, thus lives their death. Thus they live still and yet are dead, and their death is the bread of the living'. Wagner's text draws upon this exalted exemplary status of the lovers, and on the highly wrought chiasmic structures and paradoxes which the medieval poet employs to superb effect; and he used them as a dramatic and poetic vehicle for his brand of Schopenhauerian metaphysics, and as a means of exploring the German Romantic fascination with the unity of love and death.

But the medieval poem also displays an uncompromising moral realism and a clear insight into the dissembling hypocrisy of the court, where Tristan can exploit the ambiguities of language to his own advantage, until he is ultimately trapped by them himself. Wagner has retained and adapted something of this in his first act. Isolde's narration of how Tristan tricked her into healing him before coming to claim her as his uncle's bride establishes a tone of sarcasm and deep irony; as she curses him and chooses the death-potion this tone is intensified, so that Tristan, confronted with her demand for 'atonement', can only reply in obscure verbal paradoxes and dark enigmas which tax the powers of listener and translator alike. Even an audience which can hear the sung text can scarcely be expected to grasp, on a first hearing, the repeated chiasmus and the sense of the lines

> Des Schweigens Herrin
> heisst mich schweigen:
> fass ich, was sie verschwieg,
> verschweig ich, was sie nicht fasst.

What Tristan is refusing to say here is soon spoken when the potion sweeps all inhibitions away; but the orchestral score has already told us what it was, expressing the dramatic movement on a level the verbal text cannot reach.

Wagner's verse, judged purely as poetry, is not of the first rank; but it fulfils its purpose completely. The lines are short and often very forceful, but they do not offer much resistance to the ebb and flow of the long sentence units. The combination of unifying factors such as alliteration, rhyme and assonance with antithetical figures such as paradox, contrast, and chiasmus suggests a linking across the line divisions. One remembers the rhyme that expresses Brangäne's warning

> Habet acht! Habet acht!
> Bald entweicht die Nacht

in the ecstasy of the lovers' worship of night, a warning that is accompanied by what Thomas Mann called 'that ascent of the violins that passeth all understanding'. As the lovers, man and woman, Tristan and Isolde, draw ever closer, the effect of the rhymes becomes incantatory: 'ungetrennt/ohne End"', 'mein/dein/ein'.

Wagner's art forces us to attend to the text. Indeed, *Tristan and Isolde* is surely the only opera in which the heroine is heard reflecting on the title of the work in which she figures. Isolde comments on that 'sweet, small word "and" ', a word which joins together (as in the title, Tristan *and* Isolde), but which, in the very act of joining together, alas, demonstrates clearly the condition of separation, or, as Schopenhauer would put it, of individuation. Hence the protagonists' constant need to name that self which they seek to transcend. Wagner's text is therefore not merely a pretext for music: language is the only possible medium for expressing essential forces in the drama, just as the music articulates elements which are beyond the limits of what language can say.

Thematic Guide

Many of the themes from the opera have been identified in the articles by numbers in square brackets, which refer to the themes set out on these pages. The themes are also identified by the numbers in brackets at the corresponding points in the libretto, so that the words can be related to the musical themes.

[3] *Note that* [10] *grows out of the end of* [3], *and that* [15] *grows out of the end of* [10]

[4]

[5]

Lento e languido

[6]

'Poison'

[7]

Lento e languido

[8]

Lento e languido

[9] THE YOUNG SAILOR

Moderato

Fresh west - ern wind o blow us home:
Frisch weht der Wind, der Hei mat zu:

[10] *Compare with* [22]

Moderato

a   b

[11] KURWENAL

Vivace

Sir Mo - rold crossed the I - rish main, to
Herr Mo - rold zog zu Mee - re - her, in

Corn - wall he - was fer - ried,
Korn - wall Zins zu ha - ben;

39

[12]

Molto vivace

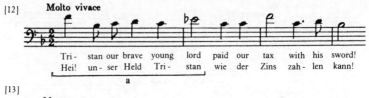

Tri - stan our brave young lord paid our tax with his sword!
Hei! un - ser Held Tri - stan wie der Zins zah - len kann!

a

[13]

Mosso

[14] SAILOR'S CRIES *Compare the double-bass phrase at the end of the Prelude*

Allegro

Ho! Ha! Ho! He!

[15a]   [15b]

Lento

a (see [3])

b

[16]

[16a] **Molto vivace**   [16b]

[16c]   [16d] **Animato**

[17]

Molto vivace

[18]

Molto vivace

a

40

[19a] Molto vivace

[19b] Molto vivace

[19c]

[20] *The Hunting Call*
Molto vivace

[21] Andante con moto
p

[22] **TRISTAN**
Un poco tenuto

That yearn - ing deep for ho - ly night
Das Seh - hen hin zur heil' gen Nacht,

[23] **TRISTAN**
Molto moderato

Oh sink a - round us night of lo - ving
O sink her - nie - der, Nacht der Lie - be

[24] **ISOLDE**
Molto moderato *tranquillo*
p

In my breast the sun is de - cli - ning
Barg im Bu - sen uns sich die Son - ne

41

[26] TRISTAN

So let us die and ne - ver part
So stür ben wir, um un - ge - trennt

[30] TRISTAN

The land that Tri - stan means where sun - light casts no beams.
Dem Land, das Tri - stan meint der Son - ne Licht nicht scheint.

[34] Molto moderato

[34b]

[34c] Molto moderato

[34d]

[35] Vivace

[36] [36a] Molto vivace   [36b] Molto animato

[37] Un poco strascinando

[38] Largo

43

[39] *The Shepherd's happy tune*

[40]

[41]

[42]

[43]   [44]

[45]   [46]

[47] **KURWENAL**

He   who   loved   as   no   man   e -   ver   loved
Der   wie   kei - ner   ge - liebt   und   ge - minnt

44

Tristan und Isolde
Tristan and Isolde

Lyric drama by Richard Wagner
English translation by Andrew Porter

The German poem follows the verse lay-out of Wagner's original although modern German spelling conventions have been adopted. The English translation follows this lay-out and consequently the punctuation of the English text is problematic. Wagner's stage directions have been literally translated and do not form part of Andrew Porter's translation. The figures in square brackets refer to the thematic guide.

Tristan and Isolde was first performed in Munich on June 10, 1865. The first performance at Drury Lane, London on June 20, 1882 was followed four years later by the first performance in America, in New York on December 1, 1886. The first performance of this translation was in Seattle in 1981; the first performance by English National Opera was on August 8, 1981.

Ludwig Schnorr and his wife Malvina, the first singers to perform Tristan and Isolde.

THE CHARACTERS

Tristan	tenor
King Mark	bass
Isolde	soprano
Kurwenal	baritone
Melot	tenor
Brangäne	soprano
A Shepherd	tenor
A Steersman	baritone
Sailors, Courtiers	tenors, basses

The first page of the original draft of Wagner's poem with an outline of the Young Sailor's Song August/September 1857 (Bildarchiv-Bayreuther Festspiele)

Act One

Scene One. *A tent-like apartment on the fore-deck of a ship, richly hung with tapestries, quite enclosed at first. A narrow companion ladder on one side leads below. Isolde on a couch, her face buried in the cushions. Brangäne, holding open a curtain, looks over the side of the ship.*

VOICE OF A YOUNG SAILOR
(heard from the mast above)

Westwards		Westwärts
strays my eye,		schweift der Blick:
eastwards		ostwärts
on we fly.		streicht das Schiff.
Fresh western wind	[9]	Frisch weht der Wind
O blow us home:		der Heimat zu:
my Irish child,		mein irisch Kind,
where do you roam?		wo weilest du?
Is this your tearful sighing,		Sind's deiner Seufzer Wehen,
keeping the vessel flying?		die mir die Segel blähen?
Waft us, waft us, O wind!		Wehe, wehe, du Wind!
Woe, ah woe to my child!		Weh, ach wehe, mein Kind!
Fair Irish maid,		Irische Maid,
you wild and lovable maid!		du wilde, minnige Maid!

ISOLDE
(suddenly starting up)

Who dares to mock me?	[4, 41]	Wer wagt mich zu höhnen?

(She looks around her, bewildered.)

Brangäne, you.		Brangäne, du?
Say, where are we?		Sag — wo sind wir?

BRANGÄNE
(at the opening)

Blue the streaks that	[9]	Blaue Streifen
rise on the eastern bow;		stiegen im Westen auf;
swift and smooth		sanft und schnell
onwards we sail,		segelt das Schiff:
and calm is the sea, by evening		auf ruhiger See vor Abend
we are sure to arrive at the land.		erreichen wir sicher das Land.

ISOLDE

What land?	Welches Land?

BRANGÄNE

Cornwall's verdant strand.	Kornwalls grünen Strand.

ISOLDE

Nevermore!	Nimmermehr!
Today or ever!	Nicht heut noch morgen!

BRANGÄNE
(lets the curtain fall and hastens in consternation to Isolde)

What say you! Lady! Ah!	Was hör ich? Herrin! Ha!

ISOLDE
(gazing wildly before her)

Degenerate child!		Entartet Geschlecht!
Shame of your fathers!		Unwert der Ahnen!
On whom, mother,	[9]	Wohin, Mutter,
bestowed you the might		vergabst du die Macht,
to command the storm and the ocean?		über Meer und Sturm zu gebieten?
O feeble art	[2]	O zahme Kunst
of sorcery		der Zauberin,
only healing draughts you can brew.		die nur Balsamtränke noch braut!
Awaken within me	[9]	Erwache mir wieder,
conquering might		kühne Gewalt;
from the bosom		herauf aus dem Busen,
where you now hide!		wo du dich bargst!
Hear my commandment,		Hört meinen Willen,
cowardly breezes!		zagende Winde!
Rise up to strife,		Heran zu Kampf
to violent storm,		und Wettergetös!

to thundering tempest	[2]	Zu tobender Stürme
clamour and fury!		wütendem Wirbel!
Rouse from its dream		Treibt aus dem Schlaf
the slumbering sea,		dies träumende Meer,
wake in the depth		weckt aus dem Grund
cruel greed to destroy!		seine grollende Gier!
Show it the booty	[9]	Zeigt ihm die Beute,
I freely grant it!		die ich ihm biete!
And strike at this insolent ship		Zerschlag es dies trotzige Schiff,
and devour and tear it to shreds!		des zerschellten Trümmer, verschling's!
And all men on board,		Und was auf ihm lebt,
the cowardly mortals,		den wehenden Atem,
I leave to you winds as a wage.		den lass ich euch Winden zum Lohn!

BRANGÄNE

(in wildest alarm, occupying herself with Isolde)

Alas!		O weh!
Ah! Ah!		Ach! Ach
This evil long I have feared!		des Übels, das ich geahnt!
Isolde! Lady!		Isolde! Herrin!
Turn to me!		Teures Herz!
What secrets do you hide?	[2]	Was bargst du mir so lang?
You shed no tears		Nicht eine Träne
at parting from father and mother;		weintest du Vater und Mutter;
nor said farewell		kaum einen Gruss
to those whom we left behind.	[4]	den Bleibenden botest du.
But you left your homeland		Von der Heimat scheidend
cold and mute,		kalt und stumm,
pale and silent		bleich und schweigend
on the voyage;		auf der Fahrt;
food refusing,		ohne Nahrung,
without sleep,		ohne Schlaf;
stern and wretched,		starr und elend,
wild, distraught.	[9]	wild verstört:
How it grieved me		wie ertrug ich,
thus to see you,		so dich sehend,
am I naught to you,		nichts dir mehr zu sein,
am I not your friend?		fremd vor dir zu stehn?
O now tell me	[2]	Oh, nun melde,
all your care!		was dich müht!
Tell me freely		Sage, künde,
all your grief!		was dich quält?
Tell me Isolde,		Herrin Isolde,
dearest Isolde!		trauteste Holde,
Make me feel I am worthy,		soll sie wert sich dir wähnen,
confide in me Brangäne!		vertraue nun Brangänen!

ISOLDE

Breath! Breath!		Luft! Luft!
Of my heart will choke.		Mir erstickt das Herz,
Open! Open there wide!		Öffne! Öffne dort weit!

(Brangäne quickly draws the curtains apart.)

Scene Two. *The stern of the ship can be seen, with the sea and the horizon beyond. Sailors are busy with ropes around the main mast; beyond them, in the stern, knights and squires are seated; a little distance apart stands Tristan with folded arms thoughtfully gazing out to sea, Kurwenal lazily reposing at his feet. From the mast above, the voice of the young sailor is again heard.*

THE YOUNG SAILOR

(unseen, on the mast)

Fresh western wind,	[9]	Frisch weht der Wind
O blow us home.		der Heimat zu:
My Irish child,		mein irisch Kind,
where do you roam?		wo weilest du?
Is this your tearful sighing,		Sind's deiner Seufzer Wehen,
keeping our vessel flying?		die mir die Segel blähen?
Waft us, waft us, O wind!		Wehe, wehe, du Wind
Woe, ah woe to my child!		Weh, ach wehe, mein Kind!

48

ISOLDE
(whose eyes at once find Tristan and fix on him, aside, gloomily)

Destined for me,	[2, 1]	Mir erkoren,
taken from me		mir verloren,
bold and fair,		hehr und heil,
brave and base!		kühn und feig!
Death-devoted head!	[10]	Todgeweihtes Haupt!
Death devoted heart!		Todgeweihtes Herz!

(laughing uneasily)

What do you think of that fellow?   Was hältst du von dem Knechte?

BRANGÄNE
(following her look)

Whom mean you?   Wen meinst du?

ISOLDE

Him, the hero,	[3]	Dort den Helden
who turns his eyes	[4]	der meinem Blick
away from mine,		den seinen birgt,
in shame and fear		in Scham und Scheue
averts his gaze:		abwärts schaut.
well, how strikes he you?		Sag, wie dünkt er dich?

BRANGÄNE

Do you mean Tristan,		Frägst du nach Tristan,
standing there?		teure Frau,
The wonder of all people,	[4]	dem Wunder aller Reiche,
that man of shining fame?		dem hochgepriesnen Mann,
That hero without equal		dem Helden ohne Gleiche,
that champion all acclaim?		des Ruhmes Hort und Bann?

ISOLDE
(mockingly)

Who flinches from a contest	[4]	Der zagend vor dem Streiche
who vainly tries to hide,		sich flüchtet, wo er kann,
fearing he brings someone, lifeless,		weil eine Braut er als Leiche
to be a royal bride!	[2]	für seinen Herrn gewann!
Is it mysterious		Dünkt es dich dunkel,
what I say?		mein Gedicht?
Go to that man		Frag ihn denn selbst,
of shining fame,		den freien Mann,
ask if he dares approach?		ob mir zu nahn er wagt?
The peerless knight		Der Ehren Gruss
whom all acclaim		und zücht'ge Acht
forgets the duty		vergisst der Herrin
he owes to me,		der zage Held,
he's afraid lest his glance meet my glance,	[4]	dass ihr Blick ihn nur nicht erreiche
that hero without equal!		den Helden ohne Gleiche!
Oh he knows		Oh, er weiss
why it's so.		wohl, warum!
To that proud one go,		Zu dem Stolzen geh,
take him his Lady's word.		meld ihm der Herrin Wort:
He must come at once		Meinem Dienst bereit
here to learn my command.		schleunig soll er mir nahn.

BRANGÄNE

Shall I request him	Soll ich ihn bitten
to attend you?	dich zu grüssen?

ISOLDE

Let fear of me	Befehlen liess
compel obedience,	dem Eigenholde
I command him,	Furcht der Herrin
I, Isolde!	ich, Isolde.

At Isolde's imperious sign, Brangäne withdraws humbly and walks towards the stern past the sailors at their work. Isolde, watching her, moves a little back to the couch, where she remains sitting during the next scene, keeping her eyes fixed on the stern of the ship. [9]

KURWENAL
(seeing Brangäne approach, he pulls Tristan's robe, without getting up)

Take care Tristan!	Hab acht Tristan!
Message from Isolde.	Botschaft von Isolde.

TRISTAN
(starting)

What's that? — Isolde? —

(He quickly recovers himself as Brangäne comes before him and bows.)

From my lady? [3]
In obedience
I will listen.
Let her loyal
handmaid tell her will.

BRANGÄNE

My lord, Sir Tristan,
she would see you,
so Isolde
bade me say.

TRISTAN

Finds she the journey long?
The end is near,
long ere the sun has set
we'll be ashore.
All that my lady commands me
truly I'll fulfil.

BRANGÄNE

Then let Sir Tristan
go to her.
That is my lady's will.

TRISTAN

See where the verdant meadows
appear still blue before us,
there my master
awaits his bride:
to him I mean to lead her,
so soon I shall attend her;
mine that honour,
mine alone.

BRANGÄNE

My lord Sir Tristan,
hear me well;
if you'd serve
my lady now
then straightway you'll attend her,
there where she waits for you.

TRISTAN

In loyal obedience
here I stand,
and serve her even now,
that lady bright and fair.
How could I straightway
leave the helm,
yet guide in safety her ship
to King Mark's land?

BRANGÄNE

Tristan, Sir Tristan!
You scorn me now.
If you despise me,
a foolish maid,
hear then Isolde's words.
I'll tell you what she told me.
Let fear of me
compel obedience,
I command him,
I, Isolde.

KURWENAL
(springing up)

May I supply an answer?

TRISTAN

Was ist? Isolde? —

Von meiner Herrin?
Ihr gehorsam
was zu hören
meldet höfisch
mir die traute Magd?

BRANGÄNE

Mein Herre Tristan,
Euch zu sehen
wünscht Isolde,
meine Frau.

TRISTAN

Grämt sie die lange Fahrt,
die geht zu End';
eh noch die Sonne sinkt,
sind wir am Land.
Was meine Frau mir befehle,
treulich sei's erfüllt.

BRANGÄNE

So mög' Herr Tristan
zu ihr gehn:
das ist der Herrin Will'.

TRISTAN

Wo dort die grünen Fluren
dem Blick noch blau sich farben,
harrt mein König
meiner Frau:
zu ihm sie zu geleiten,
bald nah ich mich der Lichten;
keinem gönnt' ich
diese Gunst.

BRANGÄNE

Mein Herre Tristan,
höre wohl:
deine Dienste
will die Frau,
dass du zur Stell' ihr nahtest,
dort, wo sie deiner harrt.

TRISTAN

Auf jeder Stelle
wo ich steh,
getreulich dien ich ihr,
der Frauen höchster Ehr';
liess' ich das Steuer
jetzt zur Stund',
wie lenkt' ich sicher den Kiel
zu König Markes Land?

BRANGÄNE

Tristan, mein Herre,
was höhnst du mich?
Dünkt dich nicht deutlich
die tör'ge Magd,
hör meiner Herrin Wort!
So hiess sie, sollt' ich sagen:
Befehlen liess'
dem Eigenholde
Furcht der Herrin
sie, Isolde.

KURWENAL
(springing up)

Darf ich die Antwort sagen?

TRISTAN

Tell me how you would reply.	Was wohl erwidertest du?

KURWENAL

This let her say	Das sage sie
to Dame Isold!	der Frau Isold'!
Both Cornwall's crown	Wer Kornwalls Kron'
and England's throne	und Englands Erb'
to Ireland's maid you gave;	an Irlands Maid vermacht,
she cannot claim	der kann der Magd
you as her own	nicht eigen sein,
for you are not her slave.	die selbst dem Ohm er schenkt.
Our hero knight	Ein Herr der Welt
Tristan the great!	Tristan der Held!
Go say "That's what he told me."	Ich ruf's: du sag's, und grollten
Then let Isolde scold me!	mir tausend Frau Isolden!

(While Tristan gestures him to stop, and Brangäne, offended, turns to depart, Kurwenal sings after her, at the top of his voice:) [2]

"Sir Morold crossed	[11]	"Herr Morold zog
the Irish main		zu Meere her,
To Cornwall he was ferried;		in Kornwall Zins zu haben;
He'd lay his tax		ein Eiland schwimmt
on Cornish backs,		auf ödem Meer,
but Morold soon lay buried!		da liegt er nun begraben!
His head now hangs		Sein Haupt doch hängt
in Irish land		im Irenland,
as tribute paid		als Zins gezahlt
by England:		von Engeland:
Tristan our brave young lord	[12]	Hei! Unser Held Tristan,
paid our tax with his sword!"		wie der Zins zahlen kann!"

(Kurwenal, driven away by Tristan's reproving gestures, goes below. Brangäne returns in confusion to Isolde, closes the curtains behind her, shutting from view the sailors, who are heard singing.)

SAILORS

"His head now hangs		"Sein Haupt doch hängt
in Irish land		im Irenland,
as tribute paid		als Zins gezahlt
by England:		von Engeland,
Tristan our brave young lord	[12]	Hei! Unser Held Tristan,
paid our tax with his sword!"		wie der Zins zahlen kann!"

Scene Three. *Isolde and Brangäne alone. The curtains are again quite closed. Isolde raises herself with a gesture of despair and rage. Brangäne throws herself at her feet.*

BRANGÄNE

Ah, how shameful!	Weh, ach, wehe!
Must I bear it?	Dies zu dulden!

ISOLDE

(on the point of a terrible outburst, quickly recovering herself)

What now of Tristan!	Doch nun von Tristan!
Tell all. Tell me precisely.	Genau will ich's vernehmen.

BRANGÄNE

Ah, ask me not.	Ach, frage nicht!

ISOLDE

Speak, don't be afraid.	Frei sag's ohne Furcht!

BRANGÄNE

In courteous phrases	Mit höf'schen Worten
he declined.	wich er aus.

ISOLDE

And when you pressed him closely?	Doch als du deutlich mahntest?

BRANGÄNE

And when I bade	Da ich zur Stell'
him straightway come:	ihn zu dir rief:
"In loyal obedience"	wo er auch steh,
so he replied	so sagte er,
"I serve her even now,	getreulich dien' er ihr,
that lady bright and fair;	der Frauen höchster Ehr';

51

how could I straightway
leave the helm
yet guide in safety her ship
to King Mark's land?"

"Yet guide in safety her ship
to King Mark's land."
"See her King Mark, I bring you
the tribute Ireland pays."

And once again I asked him
and used your very words,
he let his servant Kurwenal —

That answer reached me clearly
no word escaped my ear.
And now you know all my shame,
so hear too how it arose.
How laughingly
they sing and mock me,
but yet I could give answer.
A little boat   [13]
so small and frail,
arrived on Ireland's shore,
and in that boat
there lay a man
wounded and nearly dead.
Isolde's art   [2]
he learned to prize
with soft healing
and soothing balms
the wound that caused his torment,
with tender care she cured.
As "Tantris",
he hoped that the name disguised him;
as Tristan   [12]
Isolde knew him plainly
for in the sword beside him
I perceived a missing fragment
and it exactly
matched the splinter
that from the head
of Ireland's hero
sent home in scornful pride,
my careful hand had pried.
A cry rang out   [13]
within my soul.
Over him I stood
with shining sword,
to slay the rash intruder.
For Morold's death take vengeance.
But as he lay there   [3]
he looked up
not at the sword
not at my hand,
he gazed in my eyes.   [4]
And his anguish   [1]
wounded me so;
the sword, I let it fall then.
The Morold wound I tended   [13]
in hope that when it was mended,
for home and house he'd leave me,
Where his glances no more could grieve me!
[4a]

liess' er das Steuer
jetzt zur Stund',
wie lenkt' er sicher den Kiel
zu König Markes Land?

ISOLDE
(with pain, bitterly)
"Wie lenkt' er sicher den Kiel
zu König Markes Land?"
[12]   Den Zins ihm auszuzahlen,
den er aus Irland zog!

BRANGÄNE
Auf deine eignen Worte,
als ich ihm die entbot,
liess seinen Treuen Kurwenal —

ISOLDE
Den hab ich wohl vernommen
kein Wort, das mir entging.
Erfuhrest du meine Schmach,
nun höre, was sie mir schuf.
Wie lachend sie
mir Lieder singen,
wohl könnt' auch ich erwidern
von einem Kahn
der klein und arm
an Irlands Küste schwamm
darinnen krank
ein siecher Mann
elend im Sterben lag.
Isoldes Kunst
ward ihm bekannt;
mit Heilsalben
und Balsamsaft
der Wunde, die ihn plagte,
getreulich pflag sie da.
Der "Tantris"
mit sorgender List sich nannte,
als Tristan
Isold' ihn bald erkannte,
da in des Müss'gen Schwerte
eine Scharte sie gewahrte,
darin genau
sich fügt' ein Splitter,
den einst im Haupt
des Iren-Ritter,
zum Hohn ihr heimgesandt,
mit kund'ger Hand sie fand.
Da schrie's mir auf
aus tiefstem Grund!
Mit dem hellen Schwert
ich vor ihm stund,
an ihm, dem Überfrechen,
Herrn Morolds Tod zu rächen.
Von seinem Lager
blickt' er her —
nicht auf das Schwert,
nicht auf die Hand —
er sah mir in die Augen?
Seines Elendes
jammerte mich!
Das Schwert — ich liess es fallen!
Die Morold schlug, die Wunde,
sie heilt' ich, dass er gesunde
und heim nach Hause kehre,
mit dem Blick mich nicht mehr beschwere!

Oh wonder! How could I not see it?
The guest that I
once helped to heal?

[13] O Wunder! Wo hatt' ich die Augen?
Der Gast, den einst
ich pflegen half?

ISOLDE

Is he whom they were praising:
"Tristan our brave young Lord."
He, he was the man we saved.
He swore a thousand oaths,
eternal thanks and trueness!
Now hear how a knight
held his word.
For this Tantris
I released, undetected
as Tristan
boldly came he back;
on stately ship
so high and proud
Ireland's heiress
he asked as a bride
for Cornwall's weary ruler
his uncle, King Mark.
If Morold lived still,
who, who would have dared
to deal us the shameful insult?
Would our vassals,
the Cornish princelings,
to Ireland's crown have aspired?
Ah, woe is me!
Mine alone
the hand that drew
such shame on me.
The sword of revenge
I should I have wielded
weakly fell before me.
Now I must serve our vassal.

[12] Sein Lob hörtest du eben:
"Hei! Unser Held Tristan"
der war jener traur'ge Mann.
Er schwur mit tausend Eiden
mir ew'gen Dank und Treue!
Nun hör, wie ein Held
[41] Eide hält!
Den als Tantris
unerkannt ich entlassen,
als Tristan
kehrt' er kühn zurück;
auf stolzem Schiff
von hohem Bord
Irlands Erbin
begehrt' er zur Eh'
für Kornwalls müden König,
für Marke, seinen Ohm.
Da Morold lebte,
wer hätt' es gewagt
uns je solche Schmach zu bieten?
Für der zinspflicht'gen
Kornen Fürsten
um Irlands Krone zu werben!
Ach, wehe mir!
Ich ja war's,
[13] die heimlich selbst
die Schmach sich schuf!
Das rächende Schwert,
[4] statt es zu schwingen,
machtlos liess ich's fallen!
Nun dien ich dem Vasallen.

BRANGÄNE

Forgiveness, peace and friendship
were sworn by both our nations,
rejoicing we passed the day;
how could I suspect
that you were racked by grief?

Da Friede, Sühn' und Freundschaft
von allen ward beschworen,
wir freuten uns all' des Tags;
wie ahnte mir da,
dass dir es Kummer schüf?

ISOLDE

Oh blind all eyes then!
Hearts were feeble!
Craven soul
and shameful silence!
Yet Tristan boldly
cried aloud
what I in silence hid!
My silent care
had healed his wound,
from foeman's rage
he in silence lay;
by silence I had
saved his life,
yet then boldly he cried!
Vainglorious
in pride he stood,
loud and clear
he spoke of me:
"She'd be a prize,
good Uncle Mark;
she'd make a splendid bride.
I'll fetch the colleen
home for you;

[41] O blinde Augen!
Blöde Herzen!
Zahmer Mut,
verzagtes Schweigen!
Wie anders prahlte
Tristan aus
was ich verschlossen hielt!
Die schweigend ihm
das Leben gab,
vor Feindes Rache
ihn schweigend barg;
was stumm ihr Schutz
zum Heil ihm schuf —
[12] mit ihr gab er es preis! —
Wie siegprangend
heil und hehr,
laut und hell
wies er auf mich:
"Das wär ein Schatz,
mein Herr und Ohm;
wie dünkt Euch die zur Eh'?
Die schmucke Irin
hol ich her;

for all the ways are
known to me,
just nod, I'll cross
the Irish sea;
Isolde shall be yours sire!
I laugh: a fine adventure!"
Curse you, betrayer!
Curse on your head!
Vengeance! Death!
Death together!

[13] mit Steg' und Wegen
wohlbekannt,
ein Wink, ich flieg
nach Irenland;
Isolde, die ist Euer!
[12] Mir lacht das Abenteuer!"
Fluch dir, Verruchter!
Fluch deinem Haupt!
Rache! Tod!
Tod uns beiden!

BRANGÄNE
(impetuously embracing Isolde)

Isolde! True one!
Dear one! Fair one!
Noble lady!
Dear Isolde!
Hear me! Hear me!
Sit by me!

O Süsse! Traute!
Teure! Holde!
Goldne Herrin!
Lieb Isolde!
Hör mich! Komme!
Setz dich her.

(She gradually draws Isolde to the couch.)

Frenzied dream!
And needless fury!
Your sorrows have confused you,
your anger has bemused you!
Great honour Tristan
now accords you,
and highly he rewards you,
he gives the shining crown of Cornwall!
To good King Mark
the knight is true
while riches untold
he offers to you:
the crown he'd inherit,
throne and kingdom
renounces and lays before you,
as royal ruler he would greet you!

Welcher Wahn,
welch eitles Zürnen?
Wie magst du dich betören,
nicht hell zu sehn noch hören!
Was je Herr Tristan
dir verdankte,
sag, konnt' er's höher lohnen,
als mit der herrlichsten der Kronen?
So dient' er treu
dem edlen Ohm;
dir gab er der Welt
begehrlichsten Lohn:
dem eignen Erbe,
echt und edel,
entsagt' er zu deinen Füssen,
als Königin dich zu grüssen!

(Isolde turns away.)

And though he bears you
to good King Mark
what cause have you for sad complaining,
is Mark not worth your gaining?
Of noble heart
and kindly ways,
who matches King Mark
in might and fame?
When a noble knight
like Tristan serves him,
who would not be glad to wed him,
as consort rule beside him?

Und warb er Marke
dir zum Gemahl,
wie wolltest du die Wahl doch schelten,
muss er nicht wert dir gelten?
[42] Von edler Art
und mildem Mut,
wer gliche dem Mann
an Macht und Glanz?
[4a] Dem ein hehrster Held
so treulich dient,
wär möchte sein Glück nicht teilen,
als Gattin bei ihm weilen?

ISOLDE
(looking fixedly before her)

Unbeloved
beside that man
every day to see him!
Ah how could I bear such anguish?

[7, 3] Ungeminnt
den hehrsten Mann
stets mir nah zu sehen!
Wie könnt' ich die Qual bestehen?

BRANGÄNE

A foolish fancy.
Unbeloved?

Was wähnst du, Arge?
Ungeminnt? —

(She approaches Isolde tenderly.)

Where lives there a man
who would not love you?
Where Isolde is seen,
there Isolde
moves ev'ry heart to love!
King Mark your consort
were he so cold

[42] Wo lebte der Mann,
der dich nicht liebte?
Der Isolden säh,
und in Isolden
selig nicht ganz verging'?
Doch, der dir erkoren,
wär' er so kalt,

54

if some enchantment		zög' ihn von dir
froze his heart:		ein Zauber ab:
then I could loose that		den bösen wüsst' ich
spell which holds him		bald zu binden.
and bind him with love's dear bond.		Ihn bannte der Minne Macht.

(secretly and confidentially, close to Isolde)

Have you forgot	[2]	Kennst du der Mutter
your mother's art?		Künste nicht?
How can you think		Wähnst du, die alles
that she, so wise,		klug erwägt,
could have sent you forth with me		ohne Rat in fremdes Land
lacking the aid you may need?		hätt' sie mit dir mich entsandt?

ISOLDE
(darkly)

My mother's art,		Der Mutter Rat
I know it well,		gemahnt mich recht;
and now I praise		willkommen preis ich
her healing skill:		ihre Kunst:
vengeance if I'm betrayed,	[10]	Rache für den Verrat,
rest for the troubled spirit!		Ruh' in der Not dem Herzen!
That casket, bring it here.		Den Schrein dort bring mir her.

BRANGÄNE

It holds the balm you need.	[7]	Er birgt, was Heil dir frommt.

(She fetches a small golden casket, opens it and points to its contents.)

Your mother did prepare them,		So reihte sie die Mutter,
these mighty magic potions.	[8]	die mächt'gen Zaubertränke.
For pain and wounds	[2]	Für Weh und Wunden
a balm is here,		Balsam hier;
for deadly poisons,		für böse Gifte
healing salve.		Gegengift.

(She takes out a phial.)

The noblest draught,	[3, 5]	Den hehrsten Trank,
I hold it here.		ich halt ihn hier.

ISOLDE

Not that. I know one better;		Du irrst, ich kenn ihn besser;
I graved a marking		ein starkes Zeichen
deep in its neck.		schnitt ich ihm ein.
This draught serves in my need.	[6, 2]	Der Trank ist's, der mir taugt.

(She has risen from the couch and becomes increasingly dismayed at the sailors' shouts.)

BRANGÄNE
(recoils in horror)

The death draught!		Der Todestrank!

SAILORS
(outside)

"Ho! he! ha! he!	[14]	"Ho! He! Ha! He!
The aftermast,		Am Untermast
now furl the sail.		die Segel ein!
Ho! he! ha! he!		Ho! He! Ha! He!

ISOLDE

That means the journey's done!		Das deutet schnelle Fahrt.
Woe is me. Near is the land.		Weh mir! Nahe das Land!

Scene Four. *Kurwenal enters boisterously through the curtains.*

KURWENAL

Come now! You women!	[14]	Auf! Auf! Ihr Frauen!
Swift and spry!	[9]	Frisch und froh!
Quick and cheerful!		Rasch gerüstet!
Get yourselves ready to land!		Fertig nun, hurtig und flink!
To Dame Isolde		Und Frau Isolden
I bring tidings		sollt' ich sagen
from Sir Tristan,		von Held Tristan,
whom I serve:		meinem Herrn:
up there a flag is flying,	[9]	Vom Mast der Freude Flagge,
and gaily waves t'ward the land;		sie wehe lustig ins Land;
and in the royal castle		in Markes Königschlosse
they know the bride's at hand.		mach' sie ihr Nahn bekannt.

So Dame Isolde's asked to hasten, prepare now for the landing, Sir Tristan will escort you.	Drum Frau Isolde bät' er eilen, fürs Land sich zu bereiten, dass er sie könnt' geleiten.

ISOLDE

(after initially shrinking back in horror at the message, calmly and with dignity)

To Sir Tristan I send this reply. Go tell him what I answer: if he intends to lead me before King Mark, his master, then first he must come to seek my grace, and first atonement must be made for unforgiven wrong: he'll come to seek my grace.	Herrn Tristan bringe meinen Gruss und meld ihm, was ich sage. Sollt' ich zur Seit' ihm gehen, vor König Marke zu stehen, nicht möcht' es nach Zucht und Fug geschehn, empfing ich Sühne nicht zuvor für ungesühnte Schuld. [10] Drum such er meine Huld.

(Kurwenal makes a scornful gesture.)

You mark my words, and tell them true! I'll not prepare for landing, his hand shall not escort me; but if he intends to lead me before King Mark, his master, then first he must come here, he must beg for my grace, atonement must be made for unforgiven wrong: I'll grant him my grace.	Du merke wohl und meld es gut! Nicht woll' ich mich bereiten, [15a] ans Land ihn zu begleiten; nicht werd ich zur Seit' ihm gehen, vor König Marke zu stehen, begehrte Vergessen und Vergeben nach Zucht und Fug er nicht zuvor [10] für ungebüsste Schuld: die böt' ihm meine Huld!

KURWENAL

Rest assured, I'll tell him that: let's see what he replies.	Sicher wisst, das sag ich ihm: nun harrt, wie er mich hört!

(he retires quickly.)

ISOLDE

(hastens to Brangäne and embraces her vehemently)

Now farewell Brangäne! Greet now the world, greet my father and mother.	Nun leb wohl, Brangäne! Grüss mir die Welt, grüsse mir Vater und Mutter!

BRANGÄNE

What's that? What mean you? Would you escape? Ah, then where must I follow?	Was ist! Was sinnst du? Wolltest du fliehn? Wohin soll ich dir folgen?

ISOLDE

(quickly stopping herself)

Did you not hear? I stay here, Tristan I am awaiting. So now fulfil what I command, prepare the draught we must drink; you know which one I mean?	Hörtest du nicht? [15a] Hier bleib ich, [6] Tristan will ich erwarten. Getreu befolg, was ich befehl, den Sühnetrank rüste schnell: du weisst, den ich dir wies?

BRANGÄNE

What drink is that?	Und welchen Trank?

ISOLDE

(She takes a phial from the casket.)

Here's the drink! In a golden goblet pour it out; Use it all, leave none behind.	[1] Diesen Trank! In die goldne Schale giess ihn aus; gefüllt fasst sie ihn ganz.

	BRANGÄNE
	(receiving the phial with horror)
Can I believe?	Trau ich dem Sinn?
	ISOLDE
Can you be true!	Sei du mir treu!
	BRANGÄNE
This drink — for whom?	Der Trank — für wen?
	ISOLDE
For him who betrayed.	Wer mich betrog.
	BRANGÄNE
Tristan?	Tristan?
	ISOLDE
Drinks it in atonement.	Trinke mir Sühne.

BRANGÄNE
(throwing herself at Isolde's feet)

Appalling! Spare one who loves you!	Entsetzen! Schone mich Arme!

ISOLDE
(with vehemence)

No, you spare me.		Schone du mich,
Disloyal maid!		untreue Magd!
Have you forgot	[2]	Kennst du der Mutter
my mother's art?		Künste nicht?
How can you think		Wähnst du, die alles
that she so wise,		klug erwägt,
could have sent me forth with you		ohne Rat in fremdes Land
lacking the aid I may need?		hätt' sie mit dir mich entsandt?
For pain and wounds		Für Weh und Wunden
she sent a balsam,		gab sie Balsam;
for deadly poisons		für böse Gifte
healing salve:		Gegengift:
for deepest woe,	[6]	für tiefstes Weh,
for highest grief		für höchstes Leid
she sent the death draught.	[10]	gab sie den Todestrank.
Let death now give her thanks.		Der Tod nun sag ihr Dank!

BRANGÄNE
(scarcely able to control herself)

Oh deepest woe.	O tiefstes Weh!
	ISOLDE
So now you'll obey?	Gehorchst du mir nun?
	BRANGÄNE
Oh highest grief.	O höchstes Leid!
	ISOLDE
Will you be true?	Bist du mir treu?
	BRANGÄNE
The drink?	Der Trank?
	KURWENAL
	(entering)
Sir Tristan.	Herr Tristan.

(Isolde make a terrible effort to compose herself. Brangäne raises herself, alarmed and bewildered.)

ISOLDE
(to Kurwenal)

Sir Tristan may approach.	Herr Tristan trete nah!

Scene Five. *Kurwenal retires. Brangäne, scarcely mistress of herself, retires to the background. Isolde, by a resolute effort, recovers herself and walks slowly and with great dignity towards the couch, on the head of which she leans staring at the entrance.* [15]

TRISTAN
(Tristan enters and remains respectfully standing at the entrance. Isolde, fearfully excited, forgets herself as she looks at him.) [15a]

Command, lady,	Begehrt, Herrin,
what you will.	was Ihr wünscht.

Did you not hear what I commanded, or was it fear, fear to fulfil it, kept you away so long?	**ISOLDE** [15b] Wüsstest du nicht, was ich begehre, da doch die Furcht, mir's zu erfüllen, fern meinem Blick dich hielt?
Reverence held me in awe.	**TRISTAN** Ehrfurcht hielt mich in Acht.
You showed no reverence surely to me; with open scorn declared your disobedience to my command.	**ISOLDE** Der Ehre wenig botest du mir; mit offnem Hohn verwehrtest du Gehorsam meinem Gebot.
Obedience only kept me away.	**TRISTAN** Gehorsam einzig hielt mich in Bann.
Then I owe your master little thanks, if serving him ends the accustomed respect to his bride.	**ISOLDE** So dankt' ich Geringes deinem Herrn, riet dir sein Dienst Unsitte gegen sein eigen Gemahl?
Custom holds where I have lived that one who bears a bride to her lord avoids the bride.	**TRISTAN** Sitte lehrt wo ich gelebt: zur Brautfahrt der Brautwerber meide fern die Braut.
For fear of what?	**ISOLDE** Aus welcher Sorg'?
Ask the custom!	**TRISTAN** [41] Fragt die Sitte!
You hold to custom, good Sir Tristan, one further custom let me recall: with foes make atonement, if you as friend would greet them.	**ISOLDE** [15b] Da du so sittsam, mein Herr Tristan, auch einer Sitte sei nun gemahnt: den Feind dir zu sühnen, soll er als Freund dich rühmen.
And who's my foe?	**TRISTAN** Und welchen Feind?
Ask of your fear! Blood guilt keeps us apart.	**ISOLDE** Frag deine Furcht! [10] Blutschuld schwebt zwischen uns.
That was atoned.	**TRISTAN** Die ward gesühnt.
No, not by us.	**ISOLDE** Nicht zwischen uns!
In open field, before the folk, the old blood feud was ended.	**TRISTAN** Im offnen Feld vor allem Volk ward Urfehde geschworen.
But that's not where Tantris hid, where Tristan fell to me. He stood there lordly fair and whole; but what he swore that swore I not; for silence well I had learned.	**ISOLDE** Nicht da war's wo ich Tantris barg, wo Tristan mir verfiel. [13] Da stand er herrlich hehr und heil; doch was er schwur, das schwur ich nicht: zu schweigen hatt' ich gelernt.

In my quiet chamber,
sick he lay, [13]
with his sword in silence
there I stood.
I said no word,
I stayed my hand, [15b]
but then I recalled
a vow I had sworn, [10a]
in silence I swore I'd keep it.
And now I fulfil that promise.

Da in stiller Kammer
krank er lag,
mit dem Schwerte stumm
ich vor ihm stund:
schwieg da mein Mund,
bannt' ich meine Hand —
doch was einst mit Hand
und Mund ich gelobt,
das schwur ich schweigend zu halten.
Nun will ich des Eides walten.

TRISTAN

What swore you then?

Was schwurt Ihr, Frau?

ISOLDE

Vengeance for Morold! [15b]

Rache für Morold!

TRISTAN

Cared you for him?

Müht Euch die?

ISOLDE

Dare you to scorn me?
He and I were betrothed
that noble Irish knight;
and his sword was blessed by my hand;
for me he went to fight. [15b]
Where he was vanquished,
my pride was lost; [15a]
then oppressed and grieving
I swore a vow:
if no man avenged his murder,
I, a maid, would boldly do so.
Sick and weak [13]
I saw you lie,
Yet I delayed . . . did not strike.
And why? Oh why? You may well ask.
I gently healed you,
from your foes concealed you,
so you'd fall to the man
who had taken Isold' from you.
Now you yourself
can tell me your destiny!
When the men are all glad to obey you,
where is the man who'll slay you?

Wagst du zu höhnen?
Angelobt war er mir,
der hehre Irenheld;
seine Waffen hatt' ich geweiht;
für mich zog er zum Streit.
Da er gefallen,
fiel meine Ehr';
in des Herzens Schwere
schwur ich den Eid,
würd' ein Mann den Mord nicht sühnen,
wollt' ich Magd mich des erkühnen.
Siech und matt
in meiner Macht,
warum ich dich da nicht schlug?
Das sag dir selbst mit leichtem Fug.
Ich pflag des Wunden,
dass den Heilgesunden
rächend schlüge der Mann,
der Isolden ihm abgewann.
Dein Los nun selber
magst du dir sagen!
Da die Männer sich all ihm vertragen,
wer muss nun Tristan schlagen?

TRISTAN
(pale and gloomy, he offers her his sword)

If Morold was your lord [4]
take up again my sword
and drive it surely and fast,
take your vengeance for all that's past.

War Morold dir so wert,
nun wieder nimm das Schwert,
und führ es sicher und fest,
dass du nicht dir's entfallen lässt!

ISOLDE

How ill a turn [15b]
I'd do your master
and surely good King Mark would chide me,
if I had killed
his treasured knight;
he owes his crown and his land
to Tristan's faithful hand.
Is this a trifle,
what you have done,
bringing him Ireland's
princess as bride?
Would he not scold me
if I had slain you,
while bearing his prize
so truly back to his land?
Put up your sword,
that I once held, [13]
when furious vengeance [15a]
within me swelled:

Wie sorgt' ich schlecht
um deinen Herren;
was würde König Marke sagen,
erschlüg' ich ihm
den besten Knecht,
der Kron' und Land ihm gewann
den allertreusten Mann?
Dünkt dich so wenig,
was er dir dankt,
bringst du die Irin
ihm als Braut,
dass er nicht schölte,
schlüg' ich den Werber,
der Urfehde-Pfand
so treu ihm liefert zur Hand?
Wahre dein Schwert!
Da einst ich's schwang
als mir die Rache
im Busen rang,

59

when with measuring gaze		als dein messender Blick
my form you eyed,		mein Bild sich stahl,
wond'ring if Mark		ob ich Herrn Marke
would like me as bride:		taug als Gemahl:
The sword I let it fall then.	[4]	Das Schwert — da liess ich's sinken
Now let us drink atonement.	[6]	Nun lass uns Sühne trinken!

(She beckons to Brangäne who, terror-struck, hesitates. Isolde urges her excitedly. Brangäne sets about preparing the potion.)

VOICES OF THE SAILORS

Ho! he! ha! he!	[14]	Ho! He! Ha! He!
The mizzen mast!		Am Obermast
Oh furl the sail!		die Segel ein!
Ho! he! ha! he!		Ho! He! Ha! He!

TRISTAN
(startled out of gloomy brooding)

Where are we?	[9]	Wo sind wir?

ISOLDE

Near our goal!	[10]	Hart am Ziel!
Tristan, you'll make atonement?		Tristan, gewinn ich Sühne?
What have you now to tell me?		Was hast du mir zu sagen?

TRISTAN
(gloomily)

The queen of silence	Des Schweigens Herrin
makes me silent:	heisst mich schweigen:
for I know what she hides,	fass ich, was sie verschwieg,
what I hide she cannot tell.	verschweig ich, was sie nicht fasst.

ISOLDE

Your silence tells me	Dein Schweigen fass ich,
you would escape.	weichst du mir aus.
Say do you refuse to drink?	Weigerst du die Sühne mir?

(Renewed cries from the sailors. In answer to Isolde's impatient sign Brangäne hands her the filled cup.)

ISOLDE
(advancing with the cup to Tristan, who stares fixedly into her eyes)

You hear the cry?		Du hörst den Ruf?
We reach the goal;		Wir sind am Ziel:
and you must soon		in kurzer Frist
lead me — to Mark your master.	[10a]	stehn wir vor König Marke.

(with slight scorn)

And when we are there	Geleitest du mich,
it would be well	dünkt dich's nicht lieb,
if you then could tell him.	darfst du so ihm sagen:
"My Lord and King	"Mein Herr und Ohm,
see what I've brought,	sieh die dir an:
no gentler wife	ein sanftres Weib
was ever won.	gewannst du nie.
Her betrothed lover	Ihren Angelobten
I slew with my sword,	erschlug ich ihr einst,
his head I sent her home.	sein Haupt sandt' ich ihr heim:
When wounded by	die Wunde, die
Morold's sword I lay,	seine Wehr mir schuf,
my hurt she gently healed;	die hat sie hold geheilt.
my life then lay	Mein Leben lag
within her might:	in ihrer Macht:
she gave it me,	das schenkte mir
this tender maid	die milde Magd,
and all her country's	und ihres Landes
slights and shame,	Schand und Schmach,
she granted those as well,	die gab sie mit darein,
by you as bride she'd dwell.	dein Ehgemahl zu sein.
In glorious thanks for	So guter Gaben
deeds so fair	holden Dank

wine of atonement	[6]	schuf mir ein süsser
we did share;		Sühnetrank;

60

and so her grace I won
for all that I had done."

den bot mir ihre Huld,
zu sühnen alle Schuld."

SAILORS
(outside)

Haul the rope!
Anchor drop!

[10]   Auf das Tau!
Anker los!

TRISTAN
(wildly starting up)

Loose the anchor!
The helm to the tide!
And hold the sail to the wind!

Los den Anker!
Das Steuer dem Strom!
Den Winden Segel und Mast!

(He seizes the cup from Isolde.)

Well known to me
is Ireland's Queen
and all her mighty
wond'rous art.
The balm she gave me
eased my pain:
the cup that now I take
will cure my hurt for ever.
Now mark it well
my atonement vow,
to you I gladly swear it.
Tristan's honour
highest truth!
Tristan's anguish
keenest scorn!
Heart's deception!
Dream of yearning!
Endless grieving's
only balm:
Oblivion's healing draught,
this drink I do not fear!

Wohl kenn ich Irlands
Königin
und ihrer Künste
Wunderkraft.
Den Balsam nützt' ich,
den sie bot:
den Becher nehm ich nun,
[41]   dass ganz ich heut genese!
Und achte auch
des Sühneeids,
den ich zum Dank dir sage!
[15a]   Tristans Ehre —
höchste Treu'!
Tristans Elend —
kühnster Trotz!
Trug des Herzens!
Traum der Ahnung!
Ew'ger Trauer
einz'ger Trost:
[10]   Vergessens güt'ger Trank,
dich trink ich sonder Wank!

(He raises the cup and drinks.)

ISOLDE

Betrayed once more?
Let me share it!

Betrug auch hier?
[4]   Mein die Hälfte!

(She wrests the cup from him.)

Betrayer! I drink to you!

[1, 2]   Verräter! Ich trink sie dir!

(She drinks, then throws away the cup. Both, seized with shuddering, gaze with deepest emotion, but fixed expressions, into one another's eyes, in which the look of defiance to death fades [10b] and melts into the glow of passion. Trembling seizes them, they convulsively clutch their hearts and pass their hands over their brows [4b]. Their glances again seek to meet, sink in confusion and once more turn with growing longing upon one another.)

ISOLDE
(with trembling voice)

Tristan!

Tristan!

TRISTAN
(overwhelmed)

Isolde!

Isolde!

ISOLDE
(sinking upon his breast)

Faithless beloved!

Treuloser Holder!

TRISTAN
(He embraces her with warmth.)

Glorious bride!

Seligste Frau!

[1, 2, 3, 4, 7]

(They remain in a silent embrace.)

MEN
(outside)

Hail! King of Cornwall, hail!

Heil! König Marke Heil!

61

BRANGÄNE

(who has been leaning over the side with averted face, full of confusion and horror, now turns and sees the pair locked in a loving embrace, and rushes forward, wringing her hands in despair.)

Endless woe!	Wehe! Weh!
Unrelenting	Unabwendbar
endless woe	ew'ge Not
in place of death!	für kurzen Tod!
Foolish, faithful,	Tör'ger Treue
loving deceit	trugvolles Werk
has brought sorrow anew.	blüht nun jammernd empor!

(They start from their embrace.)

TRISTAN
(bewildered)

What dream was mine	Was träumte mir
of Tristan's honour?	von Tristans Ehre?

ISOLDE

What dream was mine	Was träumte mir
of Isolde's shame?	von Isoldes Schmach?

TRISTAN

Ah, could I lose you?   [2]   Du mir verloren?

ISOLDE

Could you repel me?   Du mich verstossen?

TRISTAN

Magic's misleading	Trügenden Zaubers
treacherous art!	tückische List!

ISOLDE

Foolish and angry	Törigen Zürnens
idle threat!	eitles Dräun!

TRISTAN

Isolde!   Isolde!

ISOLDE

Tristan!   Tristan!

TRISTAN

Oh sweetest maid!   Süsseste Maid!

ISOLDE

Truest of men!   Trautester Mann!

BOTH
[2, 7, 4, 8; 8 with 2; 5 with 1; 4]

Ah, in my bosom	Wie sich die Herzen
new hopes excite me,	wogend erheben,
ah, new emotions	wie alle Sinne
rise to delight me!	wonnig erbeben!
Yearning enchantment, [8]	Sehnender Minne
love overflowing,	schwellendes Blühen,
passionate rapture	schmachtender Liebe
tenderly glowing!	seliges Glühen!
Flames of delight	Jach in der Brust
leap in my breast!	jauchzende Lust!
Isolde! Tristan!	Isolde! Tristan!
Tristan! Isolde!	Tristan! Isolde!
All else forgetting	Welten-entronnen
you are beside me	du mir gewonnen!
you are all that I know	Du mir einzig bewusst,
glorious light of love!	höchste Liebeslust!

The curtains are torn wide open; the whole ship is filled with knights and sailors, shouting and making signs towards the shore which is seen close by, with a castle on the cliff top. [14]

BRANGÄNE

(to the women, whom she beckons up from below. Tristan and Isolde remain lost in mutual contemplation, unconscious of what is happening around them.)

Quick, the mantle,	Schnell den Mantel,
the queenly robe!	den Königsschmuck!

(rushing between Tristan and Isolde)

Wake from your dream.	Unsel'ge! Auf!
Hear where we are.	Hört, wo wir sind!

(She places the royal mantle on Isolde, who notices nothing.)

MEN
(on the boat)

Hail! Hail! Hail!	Heil! Heil! Heil!
Mighty Mark our King!	König Marke! Heil!
Hail to Mark our King!	Heil! Heil dem König

KURWENAL
(entering briskly)

Hail Tristan!	Heil Tristan,
Fortunate knight!	glücklicher Held!
Surrounded by his courtiers	[14] Mit reichem Hofgesinde
in a boat	dort auf Nachen
King Mark approaches.	naht Herr Marke.
Gladly he takes to sea,	Hei! Wie die Fahrt ihn freut,
eager to greet his bride.	dass er die Braut sich freit!

TRISTAN
(looking up in bewilderment)

Who comes?	Wer naht?

KURWENAL

The king comes!	Der König.

TRISTAN

Who's the king then?	Welcher König?

(Kurwenal points over the side. Tristan gazes stupefied at the shore.)

MEN
(waving hats)

Hail to Mark the King!	Heil König Marke!

ISOLDE
(bewildered)

What's that? Brangäne!	[2] Was ist? Brangäne!
Why the cry?	Welcher Ruf?

BRANGÄNE

Isolde! Lady!	Isolde! Herrin!
Try to be calm!	Fassung nur heut!

ISOLDE

Where am I? Live I?	Wo bin ich? Leb ich?
What did we drink?	Ha! Welcher Trank?

BRANGÄNE
(in despair)

The draught of love!	[5] Der Liebestrank!

ISOLDE
(gazing horror-struck at Tristan)

Tristan!	Tristan!

TRISTAN

Isolde!	Isolde!

ISOLDE

Can I live now?	Muss ich leben?

(She falls unconscious on his breast.)

BRANGÄNE
(to the women)

Help your Lady!	Helft der Herrin!

TRISTAN

Our bliss now lives from lying!	[10] O Wonne voller Tücke!
Joy, guile-inspired, I bless you!	O truggeweihtes Glücke!

People have come on board, others have made a gangway, and all expect the King's arrival.

MEN

Cornwall hail!	Kornwall Heil!

The curtain falls quickly.

63

Act Two

Prelude. [16, 17; 18 with 17; 2, 19a]
Scene One. *A garden with high trees in front of Isolde's chamber which lies at one side and is approached by steps. Bright and pleasant summer night. At the open door a burning torch is fixed. Sounds of hunting in the background. Brangäne, on the steps of the chamber, looks out towards the hunting party, the sounds from which gradually decrease. She looks anxiously back into the chamber, where she sees Isolde approaching. Isolde, strongly agitated, comes from the chamber to Brangäne.*

	ISOLDE	
Gone are the horns!	[2]	Hörst du sie noch?
I heard them die away.		Mir schwand schon fern der Klang.
	BRANGÄNE	
	(listening)	
No, they are near;	[20]	Noch sind sie nah;
loud and clear they sound.		deutlich tönt's daher.
	ISOLDE	
	(listening)	
Fearful concern		Sorgende Furcht
deludes your ear;	[19]	beirrt dein Ohr.
by rustling branches		Dich täuscht des Laubes
you are deceived,		säuselnd Getön,
which laughing dance in the wind.		das lachend schüttelt der Wind.
	BRANGÄNE	
By fervent longing	[2] [19a]	Dich täuscht des Wunsches
you're deceived,		Ungestüm
your desire deludes your ear.		zu vernehmen, was du wähnst.
I still hear the horns in cry.	[20]	Ich höre der Hörner Schall.
	ISOLDE	
	(listens)	
No hunting call		Nicht Hörnerschall
sounds so fair;		tönt so hold,
I hear the soft		des Quelles sanft
murmuring streamlet,		rieselnde Welle
gently flow on its way.		rauscht so wonnig daher.
If horns were near	[18]	Wie hört' ich sie,
how could I hear it?		tosten noch Hörner?
In silence of night		Im Schweigen der Nacht
like laughter it sounds.		nur lacht mir der Quell.
My lover waits		Der meiner harrt
in silence of night,		in schweigender Nacht,
as if horns still were loudly sounding,	[19]	als ob Hörner noch nah dir schallten,
you try to hold him from me?		willst du ihn fern mir halten?
	BRANGÄNE	
Your lover waits —	[2]	Der deiner harrt —
oh hear my warning!		o hör mein Warnen! —
For him a spy waits by night.		des harren Späher zur Nacht.
You may be blinded,		Weil du erblindet,
that does not mean		wähnst du den Blick
that eyes are blinded to you.		der Welt erblödet für euch?
When still aboard the ship,		Da dort an Schiffes Bord
when Tristan's trembling hand		von Tristans bebender Hand
conveyed the bride		die bleiche Braut,
scarce in her senses,		kaum ihrer mächtig,
to her husband King Mark,		König Marke empfing,
when all in concern		als alles verwirrt
turned their glances on you,		auf die Wankende sah,
and Mark so gracious,		der güt'ge König
mild and kind,		mild besorgt,
deplored so long a journey,		die Mühen der langen Fahrt,
that had left you weak and pale,		die du littest, laut beklagt':
then one there was,		ein einz'ger war's,
I marked him well,		ich achtet' es wohl,
at Sir Tristan he was gazing;		der nur Tristan fasst' ins Auge.
with spite in his eyes,		Mit böslicher List,

64

hate in his glance,
keenly he did observe him
to see if aught could serve him.
Oft I find him
lurking around.
He plans some secret snare;
of Melot, now beware!

Speak you of Melot?
Oh you are deceived!
Is he not Tristan's
truest friend?
When my Tristan must leave me,
then he is with Melot alone.

What makes me suspicious
wins him your favour.
From Tristan to Mark
Sir Melot goes
to sow his seeds of hate.
And those who planned
this hunt in the darkness
decided on so swiftly,
seek a nobler prey
than you dare believe;
their's is a cunning game.

To serve his friend
he thought of a plan;
we're helped by
Melot his friend:
and now you suspect his friendship?
Better than you
he cares for me,
he opens ways
that you would close.
So end my time of anguished waiting!
The signal, Brangäne!
Oh give the signal!
Out with torch's
final gleam!
Let night now enfold us;
call on the night.
For night pours her silence
on grove and hall,
and night holds my heart
in rapturous thrall.
Extinguish the burning light,
end now the warning glare.
Lead my beloved here!

Oh leave the signal to warn you,
leave it to show you the danger!
Oh sorrow! Sorrow!
Ah Brangäne!
Accursed was the potion!
For a single time
I strayed
and disobeyed your word.
Had I been deaf and blind,
your work
brought sudden death.
But your disgrace
all your grief and shame,
my work
my work only has caused it!

lauerndem Blick
sucht er in seiner Miene
zu finden, was ihm diene.
Tückisch lauschend
treff ich ihn oft:
der heimlich euch umgarnt,
vor Melot seid gewarnt!

ISOLDE
[18] Meinst du Herrn Melot?
O, wie du dich trügst!
Ist er nicht Tristans
treuester Freund?
Muss mein Trauter mich meiden,
dann weilt er bei Melot allein.

BRANGÄNE
Was mir ihn verdächtig,
macht dir ihn teuer!
Von Tristan zu Marke
ist Melots Weg;
[20] dort sät er üble Saat.
Die heut im Rat
dies nächtliche Jagen
so eilig schnell beschlossen,
einem edlern Wild,
als dein Wähnen meint,
gilt ihre Jägerslist.

ISOLDE
[20] Dem Freund zulieb
erfand diese List
aus Mitleid
Melot, der Freund.
Nun willst du den Treuen schelten?
Besser als du
[19] sorgt er für mich;
ihm öffnet er,
was mir du sperrst.
O spar mir des Zögerns Not!
[18] Das Zeichen, Brangäne!
O gib das Zeichen!
Lösche des Lichtes
letzten Schein!
[18a] Dass ganz sie sich neige,
winke der Nacht!
Schon goss sie ihr Schweigen
durch Hain und Haus,
schon füllt sie das Herz
mit wonnigem Graus.
O lösche das Licht nun aus,
lösche den scheuchenden Schein!
Lass meinen Liebsten ein!

BRANGÄNE
[2] O lass die warnende Zünde,
lass die Gefahr sie dir zeigen!
O wehe! Wehe!
Ach, mir Armen!
[2] Des unseligen Trankes!
Dass ich untreu
einmal nur
der Herrin Willen trog!
Gehorcht' ich taub und blind,
dein Werk
[6, 10] war dann der Tod.
Doch deine Schmach,
deine schmählichste Not
mein Werk,
muss ich Schuld'ge es wissen?

		ISOLDE

<table>
<tr><td>

Your work?
O foolish maid!
Love's Goddess do you not know?
Not all her magic power?
The fairest, bravest
queen she is,
and all the world
obeys her will!
Life and death
she holds in her hand,
weaving spells from joy and grief,
true love she weaves from hate.
A deadly deed
rashly and wildly I planned.
Love's Goddess siezed
the deed from out my hand,
the death-devoted
claimed as her own,
now all my life
is hers alone.
Ah, let her tend it,
ah, let her end it,
ah, let her guide it,
let her decide it;
I'll no more betray her:
but ever I shall obey her.

</td><td>

[2]

[10]

[2]

[10, 6]

[21]

</td><td>

ISOLDE

Dein Werk?
O tör'ge Magd!
Frau Minne kenntest du nicht?
Nicht ihres Zaubers Macht?
Des kühnsten Mutes
Königin?
Des Weltenwerdens
Walterin?
Leben und Tod
sind untertan ihr,
die sie webt aus Lust und Leid,
in Liebe wandelnd den Neid.
Des Todes Werk,
nahm ich's vermessen zur Hand,
Frau Minne hat es
meiner Macht entwandt.
Die Todgeweihte
nahm sie in Pfand,
fasste das Werk
in ihre Hand.
Wie sie es wendet
wie sie es endet,
was sie mir küre,
wohin mich führe,
ihr ward ich zu eigen:
nun lass mich Gehorsam zeigen!

</td></tr>
</table>

BRANGÄNE

Although by the spell		Und musste der Minne
of love's fatal draught		tückischer Trank
all sense of reason has left you;		des Sinnes Licht dir verlöschen,
though you're unheeding		darfst du nicht sehen,
when I would warn you:		wenn ich dich warne:
oh hear me now.		nur heute hör,
Oh hear my pleading.		o hör mein Flehen!
Let the clear beacon of light		Der Gefahr leuchtendes Licht,
burn brightly!		nur heute, heut
Ah, tonight at least, leave that light!		die Fackel dort lösche nicht!

ISOLDE

She who kindles all		Die im Busen mir
my wild desire,		die Glut entfacht,
she who has set		die mir das Herze
my heart on fire,		brennen macht,
whose smile has made	[21]	die mir als Tag
my darkness bright,		der Seele lacht,
Love's Goddess says:		Frau Minne will:
it must be night.		es werde Nacht,
Then glory shines beside her,	[19]	dass hell sie dorten leuchte,
while with your light you'd hide her		wo sie dein Licht verscheuchte.

(She hastens to the door and takes down the torch.)

Go watch for us,		Zur Warte du:
and guard us well.		dort wache treu!
The torch here	[18]	Die Leuchte,
though it were my light of life,		und wär's meines Lebens Licht —
laughing		lachend
I'll extinguish, come fair night!	[10, 18]	sie zu löschen zag ich nicht!

She throws the torch to the ground, where it gradually goes out. Brangäne turns away in consternation and ascends an outside staircase leading to the battlements, where she slowly disappears. Isolde listens and peers, at first shyly, into an avenue. Urged by her increasing desire, she approaches the avenue and looks more carefully. She beckons with her handkerchief, first slightly, then more plainly, waving it quicker as her impatience increases. A gesture of sudden delight shows that she has perceived her lover in the distance. She raises her head higher and higher and then to see better into the distance, she hastens to the steps from the top of which she beckons to the person approaching. [17]

Scene Two. *Now she runs towards him.* [19acd]

TRISTAN

Isolde ! Beloved!	Isolde! Geliebte!

ISOLDE

Tristan! Beloved!	Tristan! Geliebter!

(They embrace passionately, and come downstage. They sing alternately, then together.)

BOTH

Art thou mine?		Bist du mein?
Do I behold thee?		Hab ich dich wieder?
Dare I embrace thee?		Darf ich dich fassen?
Can I believe it?		Kann ich mir trauen?
Tristan! Tristan!		Endlich! Endlich!
Here on my breast		An meiner Brust!
Feel once again?		Fühl ich dich wirklich?
See thee again?		Seh ich dich selber?
These thine eyes?		Dies deine Augen?
This thy mouth?		Dies dein Mund?
Here thy hand?		Hier deine Hand?
Here thy heart?		Hier dein Herz?
Is't I? Is't thou?		Bin ich's? Bist du's?
Held in my arms?		Halt ich dich fest?
Am I deceived?		Ist es kein Trug?
Is it a dream?		Ist es kein Traum?
O wonder, o wonder,	[2]	O Wonne der Seele,
o sweetest, highest,	[19d]	o süsse, hehrste,
boldest, fairest,		kühnste, schönste,
holiest love!		seligste Lust!
Joy unequalled,		Ohne Gleiche!
all surpassing.		Überreiche!
Love unbounded!		Überselig!
Endless! Endless!		Ewig! Ewig!
Unimagined,		Ungeahnte,
never known!		nie gekannte!
Overflowing,		Überschwenglich
high-enthroned!		hoch erhabne!
Joyful rapture!		Freudejauchzen!
Love's enchantment!		Lustentzücken!
High in heaven,		Himmelhöchstes
earth-forsaking!		Weltentrücken!
Mine! Tristan mine!		Mein! Tristan mein!
Mine! Isolde mine!	[19d, 21]	Mein! Isolde mein!
Mine and thine!		Mein und dein!
Ever! Tristan mine, Isolde ever thine!		Ewig! Tristan mein, Isolde ewig dein!
Ever Isolde mine!		Ewig Isolde mein!
Tristan! Isolde!		Tristan! Isolde!
Ever, ever mine!		Ewig, ewig ein!
How long so far!		Wie lange fern!
How far so long!		Wie fern so lang!
How far so near!		Wie weit so nah!
So near how far!		So nah wie weit!
O foe to friendship		O Freundesfeindin,
cruel distance!		böse Ferne!
Weary hours of		Träger Zeiten
anguished waiting!		zögernde Länge!

TRISTAN

O near and distant!	[18, 21]	O Weit' und Nähe,
Harsh division.		hart entzweite!
Glorious nearness!	[18]	Holde Nähe!
Lonely distance.		Öde Weite!

ISOLDE

In darkness thou,	[18]	Im Dunkel du,
in light was I.		im Lichte ich!

TRISTAN

The light! The light!	Das Licht! Das Licht!
O cruel light!	O dieses Licht,

How long you seemed to burn.
The sun had set,
the day had died,
but all their spite
was burning still:
that fiery signal
glared thro' the night
and barred me from my beloved,
forbade me to go near her.

Thy beloved's hand
ended the light;
though my maid was fearful
I had no fear;
for I trusted in mighty love,
boldly defied bright day!

The daylight, the daylight,
the envious daylight,
the hard-hearted foe, I
hate and loathe it!
You quench'd the torch
could I quench the day
to revenge the suff'ring of lovers
and quench the day's cruel torment!
Is there a grief,
is there a care,
left unawakened
by its glare?
Even when night's
splendour had come,
light still burned in thy house,
threat'ning drove me away!

Though light was burning
within my house,
within thy heart
it once did blaze,
cherished proudly
by my own lover:
Tristan, when he betrayed!
When bright with day's
deceitful flame,
across the Irish
seas he came,
a bride for Mark to claim
and doom his true love to death.

The day! The day
that shone all round
where you shone
like the glorious sun
in highest honour's
dazzling ray,
it stole Isold' away!
For while mine eyes
beheld that glow,
my heart was crushed
by heavy woe:
in blinding daylight's shine
how could Isold' be mine?

Was I not thine
when thee I chose?
What lies could evil
day disclose

[18] wie lang verlosch es nicht!
Die Sonne sank,
der Tag verging;
doch seinen Neid
erstickt' er nicht:
sein scheuchend Zeichen
zündet er an
[16c] und steckt's an der Liebsten Türe,
dass nicht ich zu ihr führe.

ISOLDE

Doch der Liebsten Hand
löschte das Licht;
wes die Magd sich wehrte,
scheut' ich mich nicht:
in Frau Minnes Macht und Schutz
bot ich dem Tage Trutz!

TRISTAN
[16] Dem Tage! Dem Tage!
Dem tückischen Tage,
dem härtesten Feinde
Hass und Klage!
Wie du das Licht,
o könnt' ich die Leuchte,
der Liebe Leiden zu rächen,
dem frechen Tage verlöschen!
[16b] Gibt's eine Not,
gibt's eine Pein,
die er nicht weckt
mit seinem Schein?
Selbst in der Nacht
dämmernder Pracht,
hegt ihn Liebchen am Haus,
streckt mir drohend ihn aus!

ISOLDE

Hegt ihn die Liebste
am eignen Haus,
im eignen Herzen
[12a, 16] hell und kraus
hegt' ihn trotzig
einst mein Trauter:
Tristan, der mich verriet!
[16c] War's nicht der Tag,
der aus ihm log,
als er nach Irland
werbend zog,
für Marke mich zu frein
[15a, 43] dem Tod die Treue zu weihn?

TRISTAN
[16c] Der Tag! Der Tag,
der dich umgliss,
dahin, wo sie
der Sonne glich,
in höchster Ehren
Glanz und Licht,
Isolden mir entrückt'!
[19a] Was mir das Auge
so entzückt',
mein Herze tief
zur Erde drückt':
[16c] in lichten Tages Schein
wie war Isolde mein?

ISOLDE
[21] War sie nicht dein,
die dich erkor?
[16d] Was log der böse
Tag dir vor,

68

to force thee to betray me,
thy true and destined loved one?

Around thy head
in splendour bright,
were glorious rays
of fame and might,
by them my heart was blinded
and madness held me captive.
That sudden radiance
that was shed
upon my weak
defenceless head,
that blazing noon
of worldly glory,
with all its radiant
worthless story,
through head and mind
then it stole
down to my deepest
inmost soul.
And in that holy night
there I perceived a light,
unknown and unexpressed,
a vision scarcely guessed;
a vision whose enchantment
I scarcely dared to gaze on;
but when daylight shone before me,
that vision shone in glory.
It seemed so noble,
fine and proud,
that boldly and clear
I cried it aloud;
to all who'd hear
I praised in pride
the world's loveliest
royal bride.
The spite that day
had waked for me,
the envy that
destroyed my joy,
the slander that was tainting
my fame and reputation;
I would dare defy,
I swore I'd try
confound my foes who'd shame me;
in Ireland I would claim thee.

Deluded slave of day!
Deceived by day
as thou wert deceived,
I, though I loved thee,
how I suffered;
naught but the daylight's
glare revealed thee
its lying splendour
then concealed thee,
though in my heart
I yearned to love thee,
within that heart
I learned to hate thee.
Ah, but my heart was breaking,
my secret wound was aching.
He whom my love concealed
traitor he stood revealed,
there to my gaze so tender

dass, die für dich beschieden,
die Traute du verrietest?

[16c]

TRISTAN

Was dich umgliss
mit hehrster Pracht,
der Ehre Glanz,
des Ruhmes Macht,
an sie mein Herz zu hangen,
hielt mich der Wahn gefangen.
Die mit des Schimmers
hellstem Schein
mir Haupt und Scheitel
licht beschien,
der Welten-Ehren
Tagessonne
mit ihrer Strahlen
eitler Wonne,
durch Haupt und Scheitel
drang mir ein,
bis in des Herzens
tiefsten Schrein.

[16c] Was dort in keuscher Nacht
dunkel verschlossen wacht',
was ohne Wiss' und Wahn
ich dämmernd dort empfahn:
ein Bild, das meine Augen
zu sehn sich nicht getrauten,
von des Tages Schein betroffen
lag mir's da schimmernd offen.
Was mir so rühmlich
schien und hehr,
das rühmt' ich hell
vor allem Heer;
vor allem Volke
pries ich laut
der Erde schönste
Königsbraut.

[16d] Dem Neid, den mir
der Tag erweckt':
dem Eifer den
mein Glücke schreckt';
der Missgunst, die mir Ehren
und Ruhm begann zu schweren:
denen bot ich Trotz,
und treu beschloss,
um Ehr und Ruhm zu wahren,
nach Irland ich zu fahren.

ISOLDE
[16d] O eitler Tagesknecht!
Getäuscht von ihm,
[16c, 22] der dich getäuscht,
wie musst' ich liebend
um dich leiden,
den, in des Tages
falschem Prangen,
von seines Gleissens
Trug befangen,
dort, wo ihn Liebe
heiss umfasste,
im tiefsten Herzen
hell ich hasste.
Ach, in des Herzens Grunde
[1] wie schmerzte tief die Wunde!
[16c] Den dort ich heimlich barg,
wie dünkt' er mich arg,
wenn in des Tages Scheine

he blazed in day-lit splendour
within that burning glow,
defied me as my foe!
All that had shown
thee false to me,
from light of day
I swore I would flee,
and deep into night
with thee I'd fly,
where my heart had told me
delusion would die;
where deceit and lies
could make no capture;
there we would drink
eternal rapture,
and we, I by thy side,
would then in death abide.

Within your hand
I saw my death,
then I understood
what thou hadst planned;
when I realised
all thine intent,
and by atonement
knew what was meant:
then there dawned in my heart
with tender might,
the wondrous charm of night;
my day was at an end.

But ah, deceit lay
within the drink,
night once again
from my grasp did sink
no death in the potion lay,
it drove thee back to the day.

O hail the potion.
Hail that draught!
Hail all its magical
mighty craft.
Throught the doors of death
there flowed a tide,
when those portals
were open wide,
then they revealed my dream of delight,
the wondrous realm of night.
From the vision my inmost heart
did enshrine,
gone was the daylight's
false lying shine;
and night-sighted, before me
I saw the truth in glory.

By revenge the day
that you scorned was fired;
and with your sins
he then conspired.
What you perceived
in glory of night
to the empty pride
of kingly might
you were forced to surrender,

der treu gehegte Eine
der Liebe Blicken schwand,
als Feind nur vor mir stand!
[16b] Das als Verräter
dich mir wies,
dem Licht des Tages
wollt' ich entfliehn,
dorthin in die Nacht
dich mit mir ziehn,
wo der Täuschung Ende
mein Herz mir verhiess;
wo des Trugs geahnter
Wahn zerrinne;
[10] dort dir zu trinken
[2] ew'ge Minne,
mit mir dich im Verein
[16] wollt' ich dem Tode weihn.

TRISTAN

In deiner Hand
den süssen Tod
als ich ihn erkannt,
den sie mir bot;
als mir die Ahnung
hehr und gewiss
zeigte, was mir
die Sühne verhiess:
[23a] da erdämmerte mild
erhabner Macht
im Busen mir die Nacht;
mein Tag war da vollbracht.

ISOLDE

[2] Doch ach, dich täuschte
der falsche Trank,
dass dir von neuem
die Nacht versank;
[10a] dem einzig am Tode lag,
den gab er wieder dem Tag!

TRISTAN

[2] O Heil dem Tranke!
Heil seinem Saft!
Heil seines Zaubers
hehrer Kraft!
[16] Durch des Todes Tor,
wo er mir floss,
weit und offen
er mir erschloss,
darin ich sonst nur träumend gewacht
das Wunderreich der Nacht.
[16] Von dem Bild in des Herzens
bergendem Schrein
scheucht' er des Tages
täuschenden Schein,
[2] dass nachtsichtig mein Auge
wahr es zu sehen tauge.

ISOLDE

[21] Doch es rächte sich
[16] der verscheuchte Tag;
mit deinen Sünden
Rat's er pflag:
[21] was dir gezeigt
die dämmernde Nacht,
an des Taggestirnes
Königsmacht
[16d] musstest du's übergeben,

70

and lonely	[43]	um einsam
on desolate throne		in öder Pracht
I lived on shining still.		schimmernd dort zu leben.
Could I bear it then?	[16]	Wie ertrug ich's nur?
Can I bear it now?		Wie ertrag ich's noch?

TRISTAN

Oh, since we are		Oh nun waren wir
by night enfolded,	[2]	Nacht-Geweihte!
the envious day,		Der tückische Tag,
so keen and spiteful,		der neidbereite,
still may keep us apart,		trennen konnt' uns sein Trug,
yet not deceive our heart.	[16c]	doch nicht mehr täuschen sein Lug!
For his empty pomp,		Seine eitle Pracht,
and his glittering lies		seinen prahlenden Schein
mean naught, after night		verlacht, wem die Nacht
has blessed our eyes:		den Blick geweiht:
and the flickering glare,		seines flackernden Lichtes
the flash of his lightning		flüchtige Blitze
blind our sight no more.	[2]	blenden uns nicht mehr.
When for death's dark night,	[10]	Wer des Todes Nacht
loving, have yearned,		liebend erschaut,
when all her holy		wem sie ihr tief
secrets have learned:	[16]	Geheimnis vertraut:
then daylight's falsehood,		des Tages Lügen,
fame and might,		Ruhm und Ehr,
praise and renown		Macht und Gewinn,
that shine so bright,	[16]	so schimmernd hehr,
like motes in sunbeams scattered	[2]	wie eitler Staub der Sonnen
are turned to dust and shattered!		sind sie vor dem zersponnen!
And of daylight's idle burning	[18]	In des Tages eitlem Wähnen
all that remains is yearning,		bleibt ihm ein einzig Sehnen —
that yearning deep	[22]	das Sehnen hin
for holy night,		zur heil'gen Nacht,
where endless and		wo urewig,
always true,		einzig wahr,
Love brings laughing delight!	[19a]	Liebeswonne ihm lacht.

(Tristan draws Isolde gently down on to a flowery bank, sinks on his knees before her and lays his head on her arm.) [19, 16]

BOTH

Oh, sink around us	[23]	O sink hernieder,
night of loving		Nacht der Liebe,
let me now		gib Vergessen,
forget I'm living,		dass ich lebe;
bear me softly		nimm mich auf
unto thee,		in deinen Schoss,
from the world		löse von
oh set me free.		der Welt mich los!
Now ev'ry light	[16]	Verloschen nun
has lost its gleaming;		die letzte Leuchte;
all our doubting,		was wir dachten,
all our dreaming;		was uns deuchte;
all remembrance,		all-Gedenken —
all reminding		all-Gemahnen —
holy twilight		heil'ger Dämmrung
radiant blinding		hehres Ahnen
drives afar my fear		löscht des Wähnens Graus
world-release is here.		welterlösend aus.
In my breast	[24]	Barg im Busen
the sun is declining,		uns sich die Sonne,
high above		leuchten lachend
new stars are shining,		Sterne der Wonne.
to thy enchantment	[24]	Von deinem Zauber
all surrender		sanft umsponnen
and melt before		vor deinen Augen
thy glance so tender.		süss zerronnen;

Heart on heart	[25]	Herz an Herz dir,
and mouth on mouth;		Mund an Mund,
one the breath		eines Atems
that now we breathe;		ein'ger Bund;
bright desire of joy		bricht mein Blick sich
will blind me,		wonnerblindet,
and all the world		erbleicht die Welt
I leave behind me:		mit ihrem Blenden:
all that the day	[16]	die uns der Tag
lit with its lie,		trügend erhellt,
and all of its madness		zu täuschendem Wahn
I can defy,		entgegengestellt,
I, myself,		selbst dann
am the world:	[2, 24, 22]	bin ich die Welt:
love so true and noble,		wonnehehrstes Weben,
love so pure and holy,		liebeheiligstes Leben,
no more to awaken		Nie-wieder-Erwachens
dreamless		wahnlos
long awaited joy.		holdbewusster Wunsch.

(Tristan and Isolde lean back together on the bank of flowers, enraptured.)

BRANGÄNE
(from the turret, unseen)

Lonely watcher	[16, 23b, 24, 25]	Einsam wachend
in the night,		in der Nacht,
you who dream		wem der Traum
in love's delight,		der Liebe lacht,
hear my warning		hab der einen
call aright;	[25]	Ruf in acht,
my foreboding		die den Schläfern
makes me fear,		Schlimmes ahnt,
waken sleepers,		bange zum
danger's near!		Erwachen mahnt!
Ah, beware!		Habet acht!
Ah, beware!		Habet acht!
Soon the night will pass!		Bald entweicht die Nacht!

ISOLDE

Hear beloved!	[25]	Lausch, Geliebter!

TRISTAN

Let me die now!	[22a]	Lass mich sterben!

ISOLDE
(gradually raising herself a little)

Envious watcher!	[25]	Neid'sche Wache!

TRISTAN
(still leaning back)

I'll not waken!	[22a]	Nie erwachen!

ISOLDE

But the day		Doch der Tag
must Tristan waken?		muss Tristan wecken?

TRISTAN
(raising his head a little)

Let the day	[22a]	Lass den Tag
to death be given!		dem Tode weichen!

ISOLDE

Day and death	[25]	Tag und Tod
if they united,		mit gleichen Streichen
they'd destroy		sollten unsre
the love we plighted?	[6]	Lieb' erreichen?

TRISTAN
(raising himself more)

Our loving?	[25]	Unsre Liebe?
Tristan's loving?		Tristans Liebe?
Thine and mine,		Dein' und mein',
Isolde's loving?		Isoldes Liebe?
What though death should strike it?		Welches Todes Streichen

72

Death could not destroy it. Though I confronted mighty death, menacing both my limbs and my life, which I so freely to love have yielded, what though his stroke descended, could love itself then be ended?	könnte je sie weichen? Stünd' er vor mir [10] der mächt'ge Tod, wie er mir Leib und Leben bedroht', die ich so willig der Liebe lasse, wie wäre seinen Streichen die Liebe selbst zu erreichen?

(nestling his head more fondly on Isolde)

Though I should die, find the death I long for, yet how could the love within me perish, the ever living with me be ended? If love will not die in Tristan, then how can Tristan die in loving?	[25] Stürb' ich nun ihr, der so gern ich sterbe, wie könnte die Liebe mit mir sterben, die ewig lebende mit mir enden? Doch stürbe nie seine Liebe, wie stürbe dann Tristan seiner Liebe?

ISOLDE

But our sweet loving, is it not Tristan and — Isolde? The word that joins us: "and" how it binds us in loving bonds; if Tristan dies, would love then not be dead?	[25] Doch unsre Liebe heisst sie nicht Tristan und — Isolde? Dies süsse Wörtlein: und, was es bindet, der Liebe Bund, wenn Tristan stürb', [6] zerstört' es nicht der Tod?

TRISTAN

What could death destroy, what could death kill, but Tristan's ill, that holds him far from Isolde, ever, ever to love her?	Was stürbe dem Tod, als was uns stört, was Tristan wehrt, Isolde immer zu lieben, ewig ihr nur zu leben?

[41 transformed]

ISOLDE

But this conjunction "and" if it's destroyed, unless Isolde by life has been forsaken, could Tristan by death be taken?	Doch dieses Wörtlein: und — [22a] wär' es zerstört, wie anders als mit Isoldes eignem Leben wär' Tristan der Tod gegeben?

(Tristan gently draws Isolde towards him.)

TRISTAN

So let us die and never part, die united, heart to heart, never waking, never fearing. nameless, endless rapture sharing, each to each devoted, in love alone abiding!	[26] So stürben wir, um ungetrennt, ewig einig, ohne End', ohn' Erwachen, ohn' Erbangen, namenlos in Lieb' umfangen, ganz uns selbst gegeben, der Liebe nur zu leben!

ISOLDE

(gazing at him in rapt contemplation)

So let us die and never part.	[26] So stürben wir, um ungetrennt —

TRISTAN

die united, heart on heart —	ewig, einig, ohne End' —

ISOLDE

never waking —	ohn' Erwachen —

TRISTAN

never fearing —	ohn' Erbangen —

ISOLDE

nameless, endless	namenlos
rapture sharing —	in Lieb' umfangen —

TRISTAN

and rapture sharing —	in Lieb' umfangen —

BOTH

each to each devoted,	ganz uns selbst gegeben,
in love alone abiding!	der Liebe nur zu leben?

(Isolde, as if overcome, lowers her head on his breast.)

BRANGÄNE
(as before)

Ah, beware!	Habet acht!
Ah, beware!	Habet acht!
The night will soon be o'er!	Schon weicht dem Tag die Nacht!

TRISTAN
(leans smiling over Isolde)

Shall I listen?	[25]	Soll ich lauschen?

ISOLDE
(looking up at Tristan rapturously)

Let me die now.	[22]	Lass mich sterben!

TRISTAN

Must I waken?	[25]	Muss ich wachen?

ISOLDE

Never waken.	[22]	Nie erwachen!

TRISTAN

With the day	Soll der Tag
must Tristan waken?	noch Tristan wecken?

ISOLDE

Let the day	[25, 22]	Lass den Tag
to death be given!		dem Tode weichen!

TRISTAN

The daylight's menace	Des Tages Dräuen
shall we now defy?	nun trotzten wir so?

ISOLDE
(with growing enthusiasm)

From his lies ever we'll fly!	[16c, 19a]	Seinem Trug ewig zu fliehn.

TRISTAN

His dawning ray	[16c]	Sein dämmernder Schein
will fright us no more?		verscheuchte uns nie?

ISOLDE
(rising with a grand gesture)

Ever guarded by night!	Ewig währ' uns die Nacht!

(Tristan follows her; they embrace with rapturous exaltation.)

BOTH
[22, 23b, 26, 27, 19bc]

O endless night,	[22]	O ew'ge Nacht,
blessed night.		süsse Nacht!
Holy noble		Hehr erhabne,
night of love!		Liebesnacht!
When you enfold us,	[23b]	Wen du umfangen,
when we are blessed,		wem du gelacht,
how could we be wakened		wie wär' ohne Bangen
from you without dismay?		aus dir er je erwacht?
Now banish all fearing		Nur banne das Bangen,
sweetest death,		holder Tod,
longed for and hoped for	[22]	sehnend verlangter
love in death!		Liebestod!
Thine arms around me,	[23b]	In deinen Armen,
I am yours,		dir geweiht,
love sacred and glowing,		urheilig Erwarmen,
from all waking grief released.		von Erwachens Not befreit!
How to grasp it,	[26]	Wie sie fassen,
how to leave it,		wie sie lassen,

sweet enchantment,		diese Wonne —
far from sunlight,		fern der Sonne,
far from day		fern der Tage
and parting sorrow.		Trennungsklage!
No illusion,	[26]	Ohne Wähnen —
tender yearning!	[16c, 27]	sanftes Sehnen;
No more fearing,	[26]	ohne Bangen —
sweetly burning.	[16c, 27]	süss Verlangen.
No more grieving,	[26]	Ohne Wehen —
ah, expiring;	[27]	hehr Vergehen.
no more pining,	[26]	Ohne Schmachten —
night-enfolded!	[27]	hold Umnachten.
Undivided,		Ohne Meiden —
never parting,	[15a]	ohne Scheiden,
thine alone,		traut allein,
ever thine	[26]	ewig heim,
in boundless realms of rapture.		in ungemessnen Räumen
Blessed endless dreaming:	[27]	übersel'ges Träumen.
thou (I) Isolde,		Du (Ich) Isolde,
Tristan, I (thou),		Tristan ich (du),
no more Tristan,		nicht mehr Tristan,
no more Isolde!		nicht mehr Isolde!
Ever nameless,	[15a]	Ohne Nennen,
never parting,		ohne Trennen,
newly learning,		neu Erkennen,
newly burning;		neu Entbrennen;
endless ever		endlos ewig
joined in joy,	[19b]	ein-bewusst:
ever-glowing love,		heiss erglühter Brust
highest holy love.		höchste Liebeslust!

Scene Three. *Brangäne utters a piercing shriek. Tristan and Isolde remain entranced. Kurwenal rushes in with a drawn sword.*

KURWENAL

Save yourself Tristan!	[20]	Rette dich, Tristan!

He looks with horror behind him. Mark, Melot and courtiers, in hunting dress, come quickly up the avenue and pause in the foreground, horrified, opposite the lovers. Brangäne at the same time comes down from the turret and hastens towards Isolde. Isolde, seized with involuntary shame, leans on the bank of flowers with averted face. Tristan, with equally involuntary action, stretches his mantle out with one arm, so as to hide Isolde from the gaze of the others. In this position he remains for some time, motionless, staring at the men, who stare at him with varied expressions. The day begins to dawn. [20, 17; 26, 27]

TRISTAN

The empty day	[16c]	Der öde Tag
for one last time!		zum letztenmal!

MELOT
(to Mark)

Now, noble lord, I ask you,	[16c]	Das sollst du, Herr, mir sagen,
if what I said was true?		ob ich ihn recht verklagt?
I staked my head thereon,		Das dir zum Pfand ich gab,
have I redeemed it now?		ob ich mein Haupt gewahrt?
Behold him in		Ich zeigt' ihn dir
the very act:		in offner Tat:
guarding your name		Namen und Ehr'
faithful and true,		hab ich getreu
I save my king from shame.		vor Schande dir bewahrt.

MARK
(deeply moved, with trembling voice)

Have you then saved me?	[28]	Tatest du's wirklich?
Think you that?		Wähnst du das?
See him there,		Sieh ihn dort,
the truest of the trusted;		den treusten aller Treuen;
look on him,		blick auf ihn,
the friendliest of the faithful:		den freundlichsten der Freunde:
his devotion's		seiner Treue
freest deed		freiste Tat
stabs my heart:		traf mein Herz

by Tristan I'm betrayed.
Tricked by Tristan,
can I hope now;
by deceit
so deeply wounded,
how by Melot's act
can I be restored?

mit feindlichstem Verrat!
Trog mich Tristan
sollt' ich hoffen,
was sein Trügen
mir getroffen,
sei durch Melots Rat
redlich mir bewahrt?

TRISTAN
(with convulsive violence)

Daylight phantoms!　　　　[16d]
Morning visions,
empty and false.
Away! Away!

Tagsgespenster!
Morgenträume!
Tauschend und wüst!
Entschwebt! Entweicht!

MARK
(with deep emotion)

This to me?
Ah, Tristan, this?
Ah, where is loyalty
if Tristan can betray?
Oh where is truth,
oh where is faith?
From him who held them dear,
from Tristan they have fled.
What Tristan bore
upon his shield,
where is that
shining virtue now,
if from my friend it's flown,
if Tristan can betray?

Mir dies?
Dies, Tristan, mir? —
Wohin nun Treue,
da Tristan mich betrog?
Wohin nun Ehr
und echte Art,
da aller Ehren Hort,
da Tristan sie verlor?
Die Tristan sich
zum Schild erkor,
wohin ist Tugend
nun entflohn,
da meinen Freund sie flieht,
da Tristan mich verriet?

(Tristan slowly lowers his eyes to the ground; as Mark continues, his features express increasing grief.)

Oh why your service　　　　[29]
long and true
the noble fame,
the kingly might
you won for Mark your friend?
Must noble fame,
kingly might,
must all your service
long and true
by Mark's disgrace be paid for?
Say, did you find　　　　[29]
my thanks too small,
when all that you had won me,
fame and throne,
I bequeathed to you as my heir?
When childless, my wife
met her death,
I loved you so,
that nevermore
I sought again to marry.
When all my subjects
high and low,
with prayers and warnings
came to urge me
a queen to choose for Cornwall,
to choose a royal consort;
when you yourself
insisted too
that what the court
and country wanted
gladly should be granted;
Opposing the court and land
opposing even you,
with craft and kindness
firmly I refused,

Wozu die Dienste
ohne Zahl,
der Ehren Ruhm,
der Grösse Macht,
die Marken du gewannst;
musst' Ehr und Ruhm,
Gröss' und Macht,
musste die Dienste
ohne Zahl
dir Markes Schmach bezahlen?
Dünkte zu wenig
dich sein Dank,
dass was du ihm erworben,
Ruhm und Reich,
er zu Erb und Eigen dir gab?
Da kinderlos einst
schwand sein Weib
so liebt' er dich,
dass nie auf's neu'
sich Marke wollt' vermählen.
Da alles Volk
zu Hof und Land
mit Bitt' und Dräuen
in ihn drang,
die Königin dem Lande,
die Gattin sich zu kiesen;
da selber du
den Ohm beschworst,
des Hofes Wunsch,
des Landes Willen
gütlich zu erfüllen;
in Wehr wider Hof und Land,
in Wehr selbst gegen dich,
mit List und Güte
weigerte er sich,

76

till, Tristan, you had threatened		bis, Tristan, du ihm drohtest,
forever to leave		für immer zu meiden
my court and land,		Hof und Land,
if you did not		würdest du selber
receive command,		nicht entsandt,
to win me a royal bride.		dem König die Braut zu frein.
Your wish was not denied.		Da liess er's denn so sein. —
This woman wondrous fair,	[29]	Dies wundervolle Weib,
your valour won for me,		das mir dein Mut gewann,
who could behold her,		wer durft' es sehen,
who could know her,		wer es kennen,
who could proudly		wer mit Stolze
dare to claim her		sein es nennen,
and not feel himself most blessed?		ohne selig sich zu preisen?
I have never		Der mein Wille
dared to lie beside her,		nie zu nahen wagte,
my desire		der mein Wunsch
only could revere her;		ehrfurchtscheu entsagte,
she is wondrous		die so herrlich
fair and noble,		hold erhaben
and my soul		mir die Seele
was filled with gladness;		musste laben,
my foes you defied,		trotz Feind und Gefahr,
I owe you this joy,		die fürstliche Braut
owe to you my bride.		brachtest du mir dar.
When I was blest by	[28]	Nun, da durch solchen
this gift, my heart		Besitz mein Herz
grew open and soft		du fühlsamer schufst,
to pain and smart,		als sonst dem Schmerz,
there where I'm weakest		dort, wo am weichsten,
undefended,		zart und offen,
there I am wounded,		würd' ich getroffen,
have no hope left		nie zu hoffen,
that I will ever recover:		dass je ich könnte gesunden:
oh why so deeply,		warum so sehrend,
unhappy one,		Unseliger,
ah why do you wound me?		dort nun mich verwunden?
There with the weapon's	[28]	Dort mit der Waffe
poisonous edge		quälendem Gift,
that sears my brain		das Sinn und Hirn
and scorches my soul,		mir sengend versehrt,
destroying faith		das mir dem Freund
in friend who was true.		die Treue verwehrt,
My trusting heart		mein offnes Herz
was tortured by doubt,		erfüllt mit Verdacht,
so through the night		dass ich nun heimlich
I must stalk and prowl,		in dunkler Nacht
on friend's actions be spying,		den Freund lauschend beschleiche,
till I find my honour is dying.	[41]	meiner Ehren Ende erreiche?
What no heaven can heal,		Die kein Himmel erlöst,
why this hell must I suffer?		warum mir diese Hölle?
With no hope of cure,		Die kein Elend sühnt,
why must I bear the shame?	[29]	warum mir diese Schmach?
The deep mysterious source,		Den unerforschlich [furchtbar] tief
the causes of my woe,		geheimnisvollen Grund,
who'll tell me where they flow?		wer macht der Welt ihn kund?

TRISTAN

(raising his eyes to Mark in sympathy)

My sovereign,	[1, 2]	O König, das
that I can never tell you;		kann ich dir nicht sagen;
and what you ask,		und was du frägst,
that can never be answered.		das kannst du nie erfahren.

(He turns to Isolde, who looks tenderly up at him.)

Where Tristan now is bound for,	[25]	Wohin nun Tristan scheidet,
will you Isolde follow?	[22]	willst du, Isold', ihm folgen?
The land that Tristan means,	[30]	Dem Land, das Tristan meint,
where sunlight sheds no beams;		der Sonne Licht nicht scheint:

77

it is the sacred
realm of night [23]
from which my mother
sent me forth.
She had in death
conceived and borne me;
in dying then,
to the light she left me.
And the refuge on earth [30]
of her who gave me birth,
the wondrous realm of night
from which I came to light:
I offer now to thee [25]
yet I must go before.
So will you follow [22]
true and bold
and come with me Isold'!

When for a foreign land
a friend once sought my hand,
that faithless one
true and bold,
did Isolde follow.
Now lead me to your homeland,
and show me to your own land:
how could I flee that land,
by which the world is spanned?
Where Tristan's home may be
there goes Isold' with thee.
So let me follow
true and bold,
and lead me, lead Isold'.

es ist das dunkel
nächt'ge Land,
daraus die Mutter
mich entsandt,
als, den im Tode
sie empfangen,
im Tod sie liess
an das Licht gelangen.
Was, da sie mich gebar,
ihr Liebesberge war,
das Wunderreich der Nacht,
aus der ich einst erwacht:
das bietet dir Tristan,
dahin geht er voran:
ob sie ihm folge
treu und hold —
das sag ihm nun Isold'!

ISOLDE

Als für ein fremdes Land
der Freund sie einstens warb,
dem Unholden
treu und hold,
musst' Isolde folgen.
Nun führst du in dein Eigen,
dein Erbe mir zu zeigen;
wie flöh' ich wohl das Land,
das alle Welt umspannt?
Wo Tristans Haus und Heim,
da kehr' Isolde ein:
auf dem sie folge
treu und hold,
den Weg nun zeig Isold'!

(Tristan bends slowly over her and kisses her gently on the forehead. Melot starts forward furiously.)
[3, 27]

MELOT
(drawing his sword)

Betrayer! Ha!	Verräter! Ha!
My King, to vengeance!	Zur Rache, König!
Can you bear the disgrace?	Duldest du diese Schmach?

TRISTAN
(draws his sword and turns round quickly)

Who dares to risk his life against me?   Wer wagt sein Leben an das meine?
(He fixes his eye on Melot.)

My friend was he,
and well and truly he loved me;
my name and fame —
who cared for them more than he did?
He tempted my heart
into pride;
for he led those
who urged me on,
name and fame to increase them [16d]
by claiming you for King Mark!
Your glance Isolde, [2]
blinded him too:
he jealous, betrayed
me, his friend
to Mark, whom I betrayed.

Guard yourself Melot!

Mein Freund war der;
er minnte mich hoch und teuer;
um Ehr und Ruhm
mir war er besorgt wie keiner.
Zum Übermut
trieb er mein Herz;
die Schar führt' er,
die mich gedrängt,
Ehr und Ruhm mir zu mehren,
dem König dich zu vermählen!
Dein Blick, Isolde,
blendet' auch ihn:
aus Eifer verriet
mich der Freund
dem König, den ich verriet.

(He attacks Melot.)
Wehr dich Melot!

*(As Melot stretches out his sword, Tristan lets his own fall and sinks wounded into Kurwenal's arms.
Isolde throws herself on his breast. Mark holds Melot back.)* [29]

The curtain falls quickly.

Act Three

Prelude. [31, 32; 33]
Scene One. *A castle garden. On one side a high castle building, on the other a long wall interrupted by a watch tower. In the background, the castle gate. The setting is supposed to be on rocky cliffs; through openings the view extends over a wide sea horizon. The whole scene suggests the absence of a master, ill-kept, and here and there dilapidated and overgrown. In the foreground Tristan lies sleeping on a couch, stretched out as if lifeless, under the shadow of a great lime tree. At his head sits Kurwenal, bending over him in grief and listening carefully to his breathing. From outside a shepherd's pipe is heard* [34]. *The shepherd enters and looks on with interest, visible waist high above the parapet.*

SHEPHERD

Kurwenal! Hey!	[34b]	Kurwenal! He!
Say Kurwenal!		Sag Kurwenal!
Hear me, friend!		Hör, doch, Freund!
Has he not waked?		Wacht er noch nicht?

KURWENAL
(turning a little towards the shepherd and shaking his head sadly)

If he awoke,	[31]	Erwachte er,
it would be		wär's doch nur
but for evermore to leave us;		um für immer zu verscheiden:
unless Isolde	[33]	erschien zuvor
came here first		die Ärztin nicht,
for she alone can heal.		die einz'ge die uns hilft. —
What have you seen?		Sahst du noch nichts?
No ship there on the sea?	[32]	Kein Schiff noch auf der See?

SHEPHERD

To a different tune	[34b]	Eine andre Weise
my pipe would I blow,		hörtest du dann,
the merriest tune that I know.		so lustig als ich sie nur kann.
But tell me truly		Nun sag auch ehrlich,
good old friend,		alter Freund:
what ails our noble lord?		was hat's mit unserm Herrn?

KURWENAL

Do not ask me,	[31]	Lass die Frage:
you'd never understand it.		du kannst's doch nie erfahren.
Watch the sea;		Eifrig späh,
if sails come in sight		und siehst du ein Schiff,
then pipe your merriest tune!	[32]	so spiele lustig und hell!

SHEPHERD
(He turns and looks over the sea, shading his eyes with his hand.)

Lone and bare the sea!	[32, 34cab]	Öd und leer das Meer!

(He puts the pipe to his lips and goes out playing.)

TRISTAN
(motionless, faintly)

Again I hear it.	[31]	Die alte Weise —
Why wakes it me?		was weckt sie mich?

(He opens his eyes and turns his head a little.)

Where am I?		Wo bin ich?

KURWENAL
(starting in joyous surprise)

Ha! He is speaking!		Ha! Diese Stimme!
Yes, I heard him!		Seine Stimme!
Tristan! Master!		Tristan! Herre!
My lord! My Tristan!		Mein Held! Mein Tristan!

TRISTAN
(with effort)

Who calls me?		Wer ruft mich?

KURWENAL

Ended! Ended!		Endlich! Endlich!
Praise be to Heaven!		Leben, o Leben!
Sleep is ended		Süsses Leben,
and to Tristan life is granted!		meinem Tristan neu gegeben!

79

Kurwenal — you?
Where was I?
Where am I?

Where you are?
In safety, peaceful and free.
Kareol, Lord;
do you not know
your father's hall?

Ah, my father's?

Sir, look around!

What awoke me?

The shepherd's piping
ended your slumber;
he guards your herds
over there on the hillside.

Mine, the herds there?

Yours, I said it.
Yours the land,
house and hall.
Your men are true,
and served their lord
as best they could
and held the hall secure,
that you, their lord
and master gave them
to be their lawful own,
when leaving all behind,
to foreign lands you fared.

What foreign land?

Why, to Cornwall:
bold and daring,
there where you gather'd
honour and glory,
Tristan, my lord, won his fame.

Am I in Cornwall?

Not so: in Kareol.

How came I here?

Well now, how you came?
No horse carried you here,
for you were brought by a boat.
But on my shoulders
down to the boat
you first were borne: they are broad:
They carried you to the shore.
Now you are back home, at home
once more,
your native land,
your fatherland,

TRISTAN
(faintly)
Kurwenal — du?
Wo war ich?
Wo bin ich?

KURWENAL
[35]   Wo du bist?
In Frieden, sicher und frei!
Kareol, Herr:
kennst du die Burg
der Väter nicht?

TRISTAN
Meiner Väter?

KURWENAL
Sieh dich nur um!

TRISTAN
Was erklang mir?

KURWENAL
[34c]   Des Hirten Weise,
hörtest du wieder;
am Hügel ab
hütet er deine Herde.

TRISTAN
Meine Herde?

KURWENAL
Herr, das mein ich!
[35]   Dein das Haus,
Hof und Burg!
Das Volk, getreu
dem trauten Herrn,
so gut es konnt',
hat's Haus und Hof gepflegt,
das einst mein Held
zu Erb und Eigen
an Leut und Volk verschenkt,
als alles er verliess,
in fremde Land' zu ziehn.

TRISTAN
In welches Land?

KURWENAL
[11]   Hei! Nach Kornwall:
kühn und wonnig,
was sich da Glanzes,
Glückes und Ehren
[12]   Tristan, mein Held, hehr ertrotzt!

TRISTAN
Bin ich in Kornwall?

KURWENAL
[32]   Nicht doch: in Kareol!

TRISTAN
Wie kam ich her?

KURWENAL
Hei nun! Wie du kamst?
Zu Ross rittest du nicht;
ein Schifflein führte dich her.
Doch zu dem Schifflein
hier auf den Schultern
trug ich dich; die sind breit,
[45]   sie trugen dich dort zum Strand.
Nun bist du daheim, daheim zu Land:

[35]   im echten Land,
im Heimatland;

80

familiar things are near you,		auf eigner Weid und Wonne,
the sun will shine to cheer you,		im Schein der alten Sonne,
now death and wounds are over		darin von Tod und Wunden
you'll happily recover.		du selig sollst gesunden.

(He lays his head on Tristan's breast.)

TRISTAN

Think you so?		Dünkt dich das?
I know it's not so,		Ich weiss es anders,
but yet I cannot tell you.		doch kann ich's dir nicht sagen.
Where I awoke	[31]	Wo ich erwacht —
stayed I not:		weilt' ich nicht;
but where I wandered		doch, wo ich weilte,
ah, that I cannot tell you.		das kann ich dir nicht sagen.
The sun I could not see		Die Sonne sah ich nicht,
I saw no land nor people,		noch sah ich Land und Leute:
but what I saw,		doch, was ich sah,
that I can never tell you.		das kann ich dir nicht sagen.
I was		Ich war
where I have been forever	[30]	wo ich von je gewesen,
where I must ever go:		wohin auf je ich geh:
the boundless realm	[23]	im weiten Reich
of endless night,		der Weltennacht.
and there we know		Nur ein Wissen
one thing only:		dort uns eigen:
endless godlike	[16c]	göttlich ew'ges
all forgetting!		Urvergessen!
How could that knowledge leave me?	[2]	Wie schwand mir seine Ahnung?
Love came to grieve me,		Sehnsücht'ge Mahnung,
love it was		nenn ich dich,
that drove me forth		die neu dem Licht
and made me seek the daylight.		des Tags mich zugetrieben?
Then all I knew was yearning,	[22]	Was einzig mir geblieben,
my love inwardly burning		ein heiss-inbrünstig Lieben,
from darkness dread and tender,		aus Todes-Wonne-Grauen
drove me to find the splendour		jagt's mich, das Licht zu schauen,
that falsely bright and golden	[16c, 16d]	das trügend hell und golden
on thee Isolde shines.	[22]	noch dir, Isolden, scheint!
Isolde still		Isolde noch
in realms of sunlight!		im Reich der Sonne!
In daylit brightness		Im Tagesschimmer
lives Isolde!	[16]	noch Isolde!
Frenzied yearning,	[1, 4]	Welches Sehnen!
keen foreboding!		Welches Bangen!
Ah, to see her		Sie zu sehen,
how I'm longing!	[1, 4]	welch Verlangen!
Crashing once I		Krachend hört' ich
heard the gates	[10]	hinter mir
of oblivion		schon des Todes
close behind me.		Tor sich schliessen:
Wide once more		weit nun steht es
the gates are open,		wieder offen,
the streaming sunlight	[16]	der Sonne Strahlen
forced them wide;		sprengt' es auf;
with eyes that day had blinded,	[16]	mit hell erschloss'nen Augen
I had to leave night's darkness.		musst' ich der Nacht enttauchen:
I must seek her,		sie zu suchen,
I must see her,	[25]	sie zu sehen;
I must find her,		sie zu finden,
for with her alone		in der einzig
united can Tristan,		zu vergehen, zu entschwinden
Tristan find release.		Tristan ist vergönnt.
Woe again,	[31]	Weh nun wächst,
I must bear		bleich und bang,
daylight's harsh,		mir des Tages
deceitful glare;	[31]	wilder Drang;
cruel deluding		grell und täuschend
forms arise		sein Gestirn

wake my brain		weckt zu Trug
to madness and lies!		und Wahn mir das Hirn!
Accursed day		Verfluchter Tag
you shine again!	[16]	mit deinem Schein!
Must you ever		Wachst du ewig
watch my pain?		meiner Pein?
Must you ever		Brennt sie ewig,
burn beside us?		diese Leuchte,
Even at night		die selbst nachts
would you divide us?		von ihr mich scheuchte?
Ah, Isolde,	[18]	Ach, Isolde,
oh, Isolde,		süsse Holde!
when, tell me		Wann endlich,
when, oh when		wann, ach wann
will you quench its burning,	[2]	löschest du die Zünde,
when will you end my yearning?		dass sie mein Glück mir künde?
The light — when dies the glow?		Das Licht — wann löscht es aus?
When will the house be dark?	[19a, slow]	Wann wird es Nacht im Haus?

(He sinks back exhausted.)

KURWENAL
(who has been deeply distressed, now quickly rouses himself from his dejection)

I scorned her once	[2]	Der einst ich trotzt',
through love of you,		aus Treu' zu dir,
but now like you,		mit dir nach ihr
how I long to see her.		nun muss ich mich sehnen!
Trust what I say:		Glaub meinem Wort:
I know you'll see her		du sollst sie sehen,
here today.		hier und heut;
She'll come, I can assure you,		den Trost kann ich dir geben —
if she's alive she will cure you.		ist sie nur selbst noch am Leben.

TRISTAN
(very faintly)

Still burns that fiery glow,		Noch losch das Licht nicht aus,
the house is not yet dark,		noch ward's nicht Nacht im Haus:
Isolde lives in light;	[16]	Isolde lebt und wacht,
she called me from the night.	[2]	sie rief mich aus der Nacht.

KURWENAL

She's alive		Lebt sie denn,
so let that hope sustain you!		so lass dir Hoffnung lachen!
Though foolish and dull you hold me,	[45]	Muss Kurwenal dumm dir gelten,
this time you will not scold me.		heut sollst du ihn nicht schelten.
As dead there I		Wie tot lagst du
saw you lie,		seit dem Tag,
since Melot, who betrayed you,		da Melot, der Verruchte,
dealt you that cruel blow.		dir eine Wunde schlug.
The wound was grievous:	[13]	Die böse Wunde,
how to heal it?		wie sie heilen?
Your foolish servant		Mir tör'gem Manne
had the thought		dünkt' es da,
that she who Morold's	[21]	wer einst dir Morolds
wound could close,		Wunde schloss,
would surely heal the new wound		der heilte leicht die Plagen
that Melot's sword inflicted.		von Melots Wehr geschlagen.
For help and healing		Die beste Ärztin
I could send;	[19a]	bald ich fand;
to Cornwall I		nach Kornwall hab ich
despatched a friend,		ausgesandt:
a loyal man,		ein treuer Mann
he's on the sea		wohl übers Meer
bringing Isolde here.		bringt dir Isolden her.

TRISTAN
(transported with joy)

Isolde comes!	[36]	Isolde kommt!
Isolde's near!		Isolde naht!

(He struggles for speech.)

O friendship! Highest		O Treue! Hehre,
noblest friendship!		holde Treue!

(He draws Kurwenal to him and embraces him,)

My Kurwenal,	[36]	Mein Kurwenal,
my true dear friend!		du trauter Freund!
My friend who never fails me,		Du Treuer ohne Wanken,
ah, how can Tristan thank you?		wie soll dir Tristan danken?
My guard, my shield		Mein Schild, mein Schirm
in war and strife,		in Kampf und Streit,
in weal or woe		zu Lust und Leid
you're mine for life:	[36]	mir stets bereit:
those whom I hate,		wen ich gehasst,
you hate them too;		den hasstest du;
those whom I love,		wen ich geminnt,
are loved by you.		den minntest du.
When good King Mark	[33]	Dem guten Marke,
my service did hold,		dient' ich ihm hold,
to him you were truer than gold!	[33]	wie warst du ihm treuer als Gold!
When I betrayed him,		Musst' ich verraten
that noble lord,		den edlen Herrn,
then how gladly you gave accord!		wie betrogst du ihn da so gern!
Yours you are not	[36]	Dir nicht eigen,
completely mine,		einzig mein,
you feel with me,		mit leidest du
when I suffer,		wenn ich leide,
but what I suffer,		nur was ich leide,
that you cannot suffer.		das kannst du nicht leiden!
This anguish of yearning,	[22]	Dies fürchtbare Sehnen,
cruel smart,		das mich sehrt;
this feverish burning		dies schmachtende Brennen,
in my heart;		das mich zehrt;
could I reveal them,		wollt' ich dir's nennen,
could you but feel them:		könntest du's kennen:
then here you'd not linger,		nicht hier würdest du weilen,
but hasten up to the watch tow'r,	[33]	zur Warte müsstest du eilen —
with all your senses		mit allen Sinnen
searching the ocean		sehnend von hinnen
and keenly peering and spying,		nach dorten trachten und spähen,
there where her sails must be flying,	[33]	wo ihre Segel sich blähen,
the wind behind them		wo vor den Winden,
you must find them,		mich zu finden,
for with love to drive her onward,		von der Liebe Drang befeuert,
Isolde comes to join me!		Isolde zu mir steuert! —
It nears! It nears	[23b]	Es naht! Es naht
so bravely and fast.		mit mutiger Hast!
It waves! It waves,		Sie weht, sie weht —
the flag on the mast.		die Flagge am Mast.
The ship! The ship!		Das Schiff! Das Schiff!
It's rounding the reef!		Dort streicht es am Riff!
Do you not see?		Siehst du es nicht?
Kurwenal, do you not see?		Kurwenal, siehst du es nicht?

As Kurwenal hesitates, unwilling to leave Tristan who looks at him in silent expectation, the mournful tune of the shepherd is heard as before. [34d]

KURWENAL
(dejectedly)

Still there's no ship in sight!	Noch ist kein Schiff zu sehn!

TRISTAN
(whose excitement has faded as he listened, now begins with growing sadness)

Is that your song to me,	[34a]	Muss ich dich so verstehn,
o ancient mournful piping,		du alte ernste Weise,
is that your song of woe?		mit deiner Klage Klang?
Through evening silence	[34b]	Durch Abendwehen
once it rang,		drang sie bang,
when as a child		als einst dem Kind
I learned how my father perished;		des Vaters Tod verkündet.

83

through morning greyness,
still more fearful,
when the son
of his mother's fate was told. [34d]
When he who sired me died,
she died as I was born;
The mournful piping [34a]
through the pain
once sang to them
its doleful strain;
it asked me then,
it asks me now:
what is the fate before me, [34d]
to which my parents bore me?
What is my fate?
That mournful piping
plainly tells me;
'tis yearning and dying!
No! Ah, no! [16c with 34a]
It is not so!
Yearning! Yearning! [2]
In dying ever yearning,
though yearning brings no dying! [16c]
What never dies, [13]
yearning now calls
for death's repose
to the healer far away. [13, 34a]
Dying in the
boat I lay,
the fest'ring poison
near my heart.
Ah, I heard
that mournful piping,
my sails were blown by the wind
there to Ireland's maid. [34a, 34b, 16c, 13]
She healed my
wound, she soothed my pain,
but with the sword
she struck again,
the sword then she let
fall to save me; [6]
a poisoned potion
then she gave me:
I hoped the draught
would wholly cure me,
instead a mighty [22]
enchantment came o'er me: [34a, 2]
that death would never find me, [1]
that grief would ever bind me [1]
The drink! The drink!
The dark fatal drink! [46]
Ah, from heart to brain
how wildly it flowed.
No healing cure, [22]
not death itself
can set me free
from the yearning pain:
nowhere, ah, nowhere
can I rest:
cast back by night [34a, 16c]
to burning day,
on anguish and on repining
the sun will ever be shining.
O cruel sunlight [31, 16c]
searing my brain,
for me no escape
from the burning and pain!

Durch Morgengrauen
bang und bänger,
als der Sohn
der Mutter Los vernahm.
Da er mich zeugt' und starb,
sie sterbend mich gebar.
Die alte Weise
sehnsuchtbang
zu ihnen wohl
auch klagend drang,
die einst mich frug
und jetzt mich frägt:
zu welchem Los erkoren
ich damals wohl geboren?
Zu welchem Los?
Die alte Weise
sagt mir's wieder.
mich sehnen — und sterben!
Nein! Ach nein!
So heisst sie nicht!
Sehnen! Sehnen!
Im Sterben mich zu sehnen,
vor Sehnsucht nicht zu sterben!
Die nie erstirbt,
sehnend nun ruft
um Sterbens Ruh
sie der fernen Ärztin zu. —
Sterbend lag ich
stumm im Kahn,
der Wunde Gift
dem Herzen nah:
Sehnsucht klagend
klang die Weise;
den Segel blähte der Wind
hin zu Irlands Kind.
Die Wunde, die
sie heilend schloss,
riss mit dem Schwert
sie wieder los;
das Schwert dann aber —
liess sie sinken;
den Gifttrank gab sie
mir zu trinken:
wie ich da hoffte
ganz zu genesen,
da ward der sehrendste
Zauber erlesen:
das nie ich sollte sterben
mich ew'ger Qual vererben!
Der Trank! Der Trank!
Der furchtbare Trank!
Wie vom Herz zum Hirn
er wütend mir drang!
Kein Heil nun kann,
kein süsser Tod
je mich befrein
von der Sehnsucht Not;
nirgends, ach nirgends
find ich Ruh:
mich wirft die Nacht
dem Tage zu,
um ewig an meinen Leiden,
der Sonne Auge zu weiden.
O dieser Sonne
sengender Strahl,
wie brennt mir das Hirn
seine glühende Qual!

From blazing torment,
  heat that enslaves me,
  no cooling shadow [34d]
  shelters or saves me.
From all the scorching
  anguish of grief,
  can no balsam comfort
  me, bring me relief?
The dark fatal drink,
  with anguish imbued.
  By me, by me [37]
  that potion was brewed.
From father's grief
  and mother's woe,
  from lovers' tears [22]
  of long ago,
  from laughter and weeping,
  rapture and sadness,
  I have distilled
  the poison of madness.
Poison I brewed, [37, 2]
  poison I tasted,
  that moved my mind
  to limitless rapture,
I curse you, dark fatal drink! [37, 2, 16]
  and curse him by whom 'twas brewed!

Für dieser Hitze
  heisses Verschmachten,
  ach, keines Schattens
  kühlend Umnachten!
Für dieser Schmerzen
  schreckliche Pein,
  welcher Balsam sollte
  mir Lindrung verleihn?
Den furchtbaren Trank,
  der der Qual mich vertraut,
  ich selbst — ich selbst
  ich hab ihn gebraut!
Aus Vaters Not
  und Mutterweh
  aus Liebestränen
  eh und je —
  aus Lachen und Weinen
  Wonnen und Wunden
  hab ich des Trankes
  Gifte gefunden!
Den ich gebraut,
  der mir geflossen,
  den wonneschlürfend
  je ich genossen —
verflucht sei, furchtbarer Trank!
  Verflucht, wer dich gebraut!

(He sinks back unconscious.)

KURWENAL
(who in vain tried to calm Tristan, cries out in horror)

My master! Tristan! [37, 1] Mein Herre! Tristan!
Fearful enchantment,   Schrecklicher Zauber!
O love's deceit!   O Minnetrug!
O might of love!   O Liebeszwang!
The world's holiest dream! Der Welt holdester Wahn,
What is this you have wrought! [37] wie ist's um dich getan!
He lies there now,   Hier liegt er nun,
  the noblest of men,   der wonnige Mann,
he who loved as no man ever loved. [47] der wie keiner geliebt und geminnt.
Now see what reward   Nun seht, was von ihm
  his great love has won,   sie Dankes gewann,
what thanks love must ever win. [2] was je Minne sich gewinnt!

(with sobbing voice)

Can you be dead? Bist du nun tot?
Live you still? Lebst du noch?
Killed by the curse you swore? Hat dich der Fluch entführt?

(He listens to his breathing.)

He's breathing! Yes! [2] O Wonne! Nein!
He's stirring! He lives,   Er regt sich, er lebt!
and gently he moves his lips! Wie sanft er die Lippen rührt!

TRISTAN
(beginning very softly)

The ship? — Is it in sight? [2] Das Schiff? Siehst du's noch nicht?

KURWENAL

The ship? Ah, yes   Das Schiff? Gewiss,
'twill soon be here;   es naht noch heut;
it can't delay much longer. [2] es kann nicht lang mehr säumen.

TRISTAN

On board Isolde, [37] Und drauf Isolde,
  see her wave,   wie sie winkt,
  see her drink [5]   wie sie hold
  atonement's cup: mir Sühne trinkt.
  see you her?   Siehst du sie?
Say, do you not see?   Siehst du sie noch nicht?
  How with tender [25]   Wie sie selig,
  sweet devotion,   hehr und milde

85

moving o'er the paths		wandelt durch
of ocean?		des Meers Gefilde?
The waves are like	[38]	Auf wonniger Blumen
flow'ring fields before her,		lichten Wogen
gently t'ward the land		kommt sie sanft
they draw her.		ans Land gezogen.
She smiles to me rest	[1, 37, 38]	Sie lächelt mir Trost
and soothing peace,		und süsse Ruh,
she brings me now		sie führt mir letzte
my last release.		Labung zu.
Ah, Isolde! Isolde!	[38]	Ach, Isolde! Isolde,
How fair thou art.		wie schön bist du!
And Kurwenal, you,		Und Kurwenal, wie,
you see her not?	[24]	du sähst sie nicht?
away, be watchful,		Hinauf zur Warte,
you lazy churl!		du blöder Wicht!
What my eyes can see so plainly,		Was so hell und licht ich sehe,
do your eyes seek it vainly?		dass das dir nicht entgehe!
Did you not hear?	[38]	Hörst du mich nicht?
Go up and watch!	[24, 38]	Zur Warte schnell!
Haste to the watch tow'r.		Eilig zur Warte!
Are you in place?		Bist du zur Stell'?
The ship? The ship?		Das Schiff? Das Schiff!
Isolde's ship?		Isoldens Schiff?
You surely see it!		Du musst es sehen!
Surely see it!		musst es sehen!
The ship? Can you see it?		Das Schiff? Sähst du's noch nicht?

(Whilst Kurwenal, still hesitating, opposes Tristan, the shepherd's pipe is heard without, playing a joyful tune.) [39]

KURWENAL
(springs up in joy)

Be joyful! Joyful!	O Wonne! Freude!

(He rushes to the watch tower and looks out.)

Ah, the ship!	Ha! Das Schiff!
From northward it is nearing.	Von Norden seh ich's nahen.

TRISTAN

Knew I not?	Wusst' ich's nicht?
Said I not?	Sagt' ich's nicht,
She is alive	dass sie noch lebt,
and bringing me life!	noch Leben mir webt?
Only Isolde	Die mir Isolde
the world holds for me;	einzig enthält,
how could Isolde	wie wär' Isolde
from it be free?	mir aus der Welt?

KURWENAL
(shouting for joy) [39]

Heiha! Heiha!	Heiha! Heiha!
See her bravely sailing!	Wie es mutig steuert!
The friendly wind swelling the sail.	Wie stark der Segel sich bläht!
See her race! See her fly!	Wie es jagt! Wie es fliegt!

TRISTAN

What flag is she flying?	Die Flagge? Die Flagge?

KURWENAL

The flag of rejoicing	Der Freude Flagge
at the masthead, cheerful and bright.	am Wimpel lustig und hell.

TRISTAN

Hahei! Of rejoicing!	Hahei!! Der Freude!
Bright in daylight	Hell am Tage
I'll see Isolde!	zu mir Isolde!
Isolde to me!	Isolde zu mir!
Is she in sight?	Siehst du sie selbst?

KURWENAL

The ship has passed	Jetzt schwand das Schiff
under the cliff.	hinter dem Fels.

86

Beyond the reef?		**TRISTAN** Hinter dem Riff?
Danger is there.	[24]	Bringt es Gefahr?
There breakers are raging,	[inverted]	Dort wütet die Brandung,
ships have been shattered!		scheitern die Schiffe!
And who's at the helm?		Das Steuer, wer führt's?
		KURWENAL
The trustiest seaman.		Der sicherste Seemann.
		TRISTAN
Will he betray?		Verriet er mich?
One in Melot's employ?		Wär' er Melots Genoss?
		KURWENAL
Trust him like me.		Trau ihm wie mir!
		TRISTAN
You're treacherous too!		Verräter auch du!
Unfaithful!		Unsel'ger!
Now can you see her?		Siehst du sie wieder?
		KURWENAL
Not yet.		Noch nicht.
		TRISTAN
She's lost then!		Verloren!
		KURWENAL
Heiha! Heihahaha!	[39]	Heiha! Heihahaha!
They're by. They're by!		Vorbei! Vorbei!
Safely they're by!		Glücklich vorbei!
		TRISTAN *(shouting for joy)*
Heihahaha! Kurwenal!		Heihaha! Kurwenal,
Truest of friends!	[38]	treuester Freund!
All I have and hold		All mein Hab und Gut
today I bequeath to you.		vererb ich noch heute.
		KURWENAL
She flies like the wind.		Sie nahen im Flug.
		TRISTAN
Now can you see her?		Siehst du sie endlich?
See my Isolde?		Siehst du Isolde?
		KURWENAL
It's she! She waves!	[24]	Sie ist's! Sie winkt!
		TRISTAN
Isolde my bride!		O seligstes Weib!
		KURWENAL
In harbour they land!		Im Hafen der Kiel!
Isolde — ah!		Isolde, ha!
She gives a leap,		Mit einem Sprung
springs from the deck on shore.		springt sie vom Bord ans Land.
		TRISTAN
Then down from the watch tow'r,		Herab von der Warte,
stop idle gaping!		müssiger Gaffer!
Go down! Go down		Hinab! Hinab
to the shore!		an den Strand!
Help her! Help my Isolde.		Hilf ihr! Hilf meiner Frau!
		KURWENAL
I'll bring her to you:		Sie trag ich herauf:
Safely I'll bear her.		trau meinen Armen!
But you, Tristan,		Doch du, Tristan,
rest here quiet on your couch.		bleib mir treulich am Bett!

Scene Two. *Kurwenal hastens away. Tristan tosses on his couch in feverish excitement.*

		TRISTAN
O blessed sunlight!	[24]	O diese Sonne!
Ah blessed day!	[21]	Ha, dieser Tag!
Hail to the joyful	[22]	Ha, dieser Wonne
sunniest day.		sonnigster Tag!

87

Turbulent blood,	[8]	Jagendes Blut,
jubilant heart!		jauchzender Mut!
Joy without measure,		Lust ohne Massen,
rapturous pleasure!	[8, 24]	freudiges Rasen!
To this bed chained fast		Auf des Lagers Bann
how can I bear them?		wie sie ertragen?
So up and away,	[25]	Wohlauf und daran,
where the hearts are beating!		wo die Herzen schlagen!
Tristan the knight,		Tristan, der Held,
rejoicing in night,		in jubelnder Kraft
has vanquished death		hat sich vom Tod
itself today.		emporgerafft!

(He stands up.)

Once bleeding and wounded	[24]	Mit blutender Wunde
I fought and conquered Morold,		bekämpft' ich einst Morolden,
now bleeding and wounded	[38]	mit blutender Wunde
today I capture Isolde!		erjag ich mir heut Isolden!

(He tears the bandage from his wound.)

Heia my blood	[25]	Heia, mein Blut!
Freely you flow now.		Lustig nun fliesse!

(He springs from the couch and staggers forward.)

She who can close		Die mir die Wunde
my wound forever,		auf ewig schliesse —
she comes like a queen,		sie naht wie ein Held,
she comes here to heal.		sie naht mir zum Heil!
Dissolve O world,		Vergeh die Welt
as I hasten to her.		meiner jauchzenden Eil'!

(He staggers to the middle of the stage.)

ISOLDE
(outside)

Tristan! Beloved!	[18]	Tristan! Geliebter!

TRISTAN
(in extreme excitement)

What, hear I the light?		Wie, hör ich das Licht!
The torch light, ah!		Die Leuchte, ha!
The torch now is out.		Die Leuchte verlischt!
To her! To her!		Zu ihr! Zu ihr!

(Isolde hastens in breathlessly. Tristan, nearly fainting, rushes towards her. [18, 24, 10] In the middle of the stage they meet; she receives him in her arms, where he sinks slowly to the ground.)

ISOLDE

Tristan! Ah!	[1, 2, 3]	Tristan, Ha!

TRISTAN
(turning his eyes on Isolde)

Isolde!	[4]	Isolde!

(He dies.)

ISOLDE

Ah! It's me, it's me,		Ha! Ich bin's, ich bin's,
sweet dear friend!		süssester Freund!
Wake and hear once more		Auf, noch einmal
when I call!		hör meinen Ruf!
Isolde calls;		Isolde ruft:
Isolde came,		Isolde kam,
with Tristan she would die now!	[40]	mit Tristan treu zu sterben!
Deaf to my cry?	[15a]	Bleibst du mir stumm?
Grant me one moment		Nur eine Stunde,
one single moment,		nur eine Stunde
open your eyes!		bleibe mir wach!
The dreary days	[33]	So bange Tage
I waited in yearning		wachte sie sehnend,
to spend one hour with		um eine Stunde
you close beside me:		mit dir noch zu wachen:
you'd cheat Isolde,		betrügt Isolden,
deprived by Tristan		betrügt sie Tristan
of even this one single		um dieses einzige,

ever-fleeting	[22, 40, 15a]	ewig kurze,
final worldly joy?		letzte Weltenglück?
You're wounded? Where?		Die Wunde? Wo?
Ah, let me heal it.		Lass sie mich heilen!
In joy then we'll share		Dass wonnig und hehr
the night together;	[26, 27]	die Nacht wir teilen;
wounds must not kill you,		nicht an der Wunde,
not a wound received in strife:		an der Wunde stirb mir nicht:
but let us united		uns beiden vereint
leave now the light of life!	[5, 6]	erlösche das Lebenslicht!
All broken your glance!	[40, 15a]	Gebrochen der Blick!
Still your heart.		Still das Herz!
Have you no fleeting		Nicht eines Atems
breath for me?		flücht'ges Wehn! —
Must I in sorrow		Muss sie nun jammernd
linger here.		vor dir stehn.
I who joyful came to wed you	[27]	die sich wonnig dir zu vermählen
boldly over the sea?		mutig kam übers Meer?
Too late!		Zu spät!
Treacherous man!	[40]	Trotziger Mann!
Treating me so		Strafst du mich so
with cruellest ban?		mit härtestem Bann?
Ah, no relief		Ganz ohne Huld
for my anguished grief?		meiner Leidensschuld?
Deaf to my pleading,		Nicht meine Klagen
silent, unheeding?	[27]	darf ich dir sagen?
One moment, ah!		Nur einmal, ach!
Oh, wake once more!		Nur einmal noch! —
Tristan! — Ah!	[40]	Tristan! — Ha!
Look! — He wakes!		Horch! Er wacht!
Beloved —	[26]	Geliebter!

(She sinks down on the body, unconscious.)

Scene Three. *Kurwenal, who re-entered close behind Isolde, has remained by the entrance, speechless and petrified, gazing motionless at Tristan. From below is now heard the dull murmur of voices and the clash of weapons. The shepherd climbs over the wall.*

SHEPHERD
(coming hastily and softly to Kurwenal)

Kurwenal! Hear!	[34d]	Kurwenal! Hör!
Another ship.		Ein zweites Schiff.

(Kurwenal starts up quickly and looks over the battlements, while the shepherd gazes, deeply moved, on Tristan and Isolde.)

KURWENAL

Hell and fury!	[35a]	Tod und Hölle!

(in a burst of anger)

All give a hand!		Alles zur Hand!
Mark and Melot		Marke und Melot
see where they stand.		hab ich erkannt.
Weapons and stones!		Waffen und Steine!
Help me! The gate!	[36]	Hilf mir! Ans Tor!

(He hastens with the shepherd to the door which both try quickly to barricade.)

THE STEERSMAN
(rushing in)

Mark has arrived	[34c]	Marke mir nach
with knights and men.		mit Mann und Volk:
In vain we fight;		vergebne Wehr!
we are outnumbered.		Bewältigt sind wir.

KURWENAL

Stay here and help!	Stell dich und hilf!
While life is left in me	Solang ich lebe,
none shall dare to intrude!	lugt mir keiner herein!

BRANGÄNE
(outside, from below)

Isolde! Lady!	Isolde, Herrin!

Brangäne's call?	**KURWENAL**	Brangänens Ruf?
	(calling down)	
What seek you here?		Was suchst du hier?
	BRANGÄNE	
Open, Kurwenal!		Schliess nicht, Kurwenal!
Where is Isolde?		Wo ist Isolde?
	KURWENAL	
Betrayed by you too?		Verrät'rin auch du?
Curses upon you!		Weh dir, Verruchte!
	MELOT	
	(outside)	
Get back you fool.		Zurück, du Tor!
Don't bar the way!		Stemm dich nicht dort!
	KURWENAL	
	(laughing with rage)	
Heiahaha! The day	[36]	Heiahaha dem Tag,
has come when I slay you.		an dem ich dich treffe!

(Melot, with armed men, appears in the gateway. Kurwenal throws himself upon him and strikes him to the ground.)

Die, treacherous cur!	[35a]	Stirb, schändlicher Wicht!
	MELOT	
Tristan, Tristan!		Weh mir, Tristan!
	(He dies) [34d]	
	BRANGÄNE	
	(still outside)	
Kurwenal! Kurwenal!		Kurwenal, Wütender!
Hear, you're mistaken!		Hör, du betrügst dich.
	KURWENAL	
Treacherous maid!		Treulose Magd!
	(to his men)	
Come! Follow!	[45]	Drauf! Mir nach!
Drive them away!		Werft sie zurück!
	(They fight.)	
	MARK	
	(outside)	
Hold you reckless man!		Halte, Rasender!
Are you demented?		Bist du von Sinnen?
	KURWENAL	
Here death rules alone!		Hier wütet der Tod!
Naught else awaits you	[37]	Nichts andres, König,
King, if you enter:		ist hier zu holen:
so if you seek it, come on!		willst du ihn kiesen, so komm!

(He attacks Mark and his followers.) [36, 34c]

	MARK	
Go back! Wild madman!		Zurück, Wahnsinniger!

BRANGÄNE
(who has climbed over the wall at the side and hastens to the front)

Isolde! Lady!	[36]	Isolde! Herrin!
Joy and life!		Glück und Heil!
What see I? Ha!		Was seh ich? Ha!
Live you? Isolde!	[40]	Lebst du? Isolde!

(She attends to Isolde.)

MARK
(who with his followers has driven Kurwenal back from the gate and forced his way in)

O needless rage!	O Trug und Wahn!
Tristan, where are you?	Tristan, wo bist du?

KURWENAL
(fatally wounded, totters before Mark to the front)

He lies there here	Da liegt er —
where I'm lying!	hier — wo ich — liege!

(He collapses at Tristan's feet.)

90

	MARK	
Tristan! Tristan!	[40]	Tristan! Tristan!
Isolde! Woe!		Isolde! Weh!

KURWENAL

(trying to grasp Tristan's hand)

Tristan! Master!		Tristan, Trauter,
Chide me not,		schilt mich nicht,
I, your true one, meet you here!		dass der Treue auch mitkommt!

(He dies.) [36, 35, 2]

MARK

Death all round me!		Tot denn alles!
All are dead!	[40]	Alles tot!
My friend! My Tristan!	[29]	Mein Held, mein Tristan!
Truest of friends!		Trautester Freund,
Today, once more		auch heute noch
must you betray your kinsman?		musst du den Freund verraten?
Here where he comes		Heut, wo er kommt
to bring you proof of how he trusts you?		dir höchste Treu' zu bewähren?
Awaken! Awaken!		Erwache! Erwache!
Awaken at my sorrow!		Erwache meinem Jammer!
You faithless, faithful friend!	[40, 27]	Du treulos treuster Freund!

(He kneels, sobbing over the bodies.)
[26 in F]

BRANGÄNE

(who has revived Isolde in her arms)

She wakes! She lives!	[1, 2]	Sie wacht! Sie lebt!
Isolde! Hear me,		Isolde! Hör mich,
forgive your Brangäne!		vernimm meine Sühne!
The drink and its secret		Des Trankes Geheimnis
I told to King Mark;		entdeckt' ich dem König:
and so he set out		mit sorgender Eil'
over the sea		stach er in See,
eager to find you		dich zu erreichen,
and to renounce you,		dir zu entsagen,
bestow your hand on his friend.	[26 in Gb]	dir zuzuführen den Freund.

MARK

O why, Isolde,		Warum, Isolde,
why this to me?		warum mir das?
When I heard the truth,		Da hell mir enthüllt,
I, at last, understood it all,		was zuvor ich nicht fassen konnt',
rejoicing when I learned		wie selig, dass den Freund
my friend was free from blame!		ich frei von Schuld da fand!
To him you love		Dem holden Mann
I would unite you,		dich zu vermählen,
my swiftest vessel		mit vollen Segeln
flew in your wake.		flog ich dir nach.
But ill fortune		Doch Unglückes
followed me,		Ungestüm,
overtaking the peace I bring!		wie erreicht es, wer Frieden bringt?
I swelled the harvest of death.		Die Ernte mehrt' ich dem Tod,
My haste garner'd but grief!		der Wahn häufte die Not!

BRANGÄNE

Hear you us not?	[26 in G]	Hörst du uns nicht?
Isolde! Dear one!		Isolde! Traute!
Reply to your faithful maid.	.	Vernimmst du die Treue nicht?

(Isolde, who has heard nothing around her, fixes her eyes with growing ecstasy on Tristan's body.)

ISOLDE

Mildly, gently,	[26 in Ab]	Mild und leise
see him smiling,		wie er lächelt,
see his eyes		wie das Auge
softly open.		hold er öffnet —
Ah behold him!		seht ihr's, Freunde?
See you not?		Seht ihr's nicht?

Ever brighter,		Immer lichter
brightly shining		wie er leuchtet,
borne in starlight		sternumstrahlet
high above?		hoch sich hebt?
See you not?		Seht ihr's nicht?
How his heart		Wie das Herz ihm
so proudly swells,		mutig schwillt,
full and bold		voll und hehr
it throbs in his breast?		im Busen ihm quillt?
Gentle breathing	[27]	Wie den Lippen,
stirs his mouth,		wonnig mild,
ah, how calmly		süsser Atem
soft his breath: —		sanft entweht —
See him, friends!	[15a]	Freunde! Seht!
Feel and see you not?		Fühlt und seht ihr's nicht?
Can it be that	[26]	Hör ich nur
I alone		diese Weise,
hear this wondrous,		die so wunder-
glorious tone,		voll und leise,
softly stealing,	[27]	Wonne klagend,
all revealing,		alles sagend,
mildly glowing,		mild versöhnend
from him flowing		aus ihm tönend,
thro' me pouring,	[15a]	in mich dringet,
rising, soaring,		auf sich schwinget,
boldly singing,		hold erhallend
round me ringing?		um mich klinget?
Brighter growing,	[19b]	Heller schallend,
o'er me flowing,		mich umwallend,
are they waves	[19c]	sind es Wellen
of tender radiance?		sanfter Lüfte?
Are they clouds		Sind es Wogen
of wonderful fragrance?		wonniger Düfte?
They are rising		Wie sie schwellen,
high around me,		mich umrauschen,
shall I breathe them,		soll ich atmen,
shall I hear them?		soll ich lauschen?
Shall I taste them,		Soll ich schlürfen,
dive beneath them?		untertauchen?
Drown in tide		Süss in Düften
of melting sweetness?		mich verhauchen?
In the rapturous swell		In dem wogenden Schwall
in the turbulent spell,		in dem tönenden Schall
in the welcoming wave,		in des Welt-Atems
holding all.	[16, 19b]	wehendem All —
I'm sinking,		ertrinken
I'm drowning,		versinken —
unaware,		unbewusst —
Highest love!	[2]	höchste Lust!

(Isolde sighs in ecstasy, held in Brangäne's arms, and sinks upon Tristan's body. Profound emotion and grief of the bystanders. Mark calls down a blessing on the dead.) [2]

Curtain.

Act III at Bayreuth, 1962. At the very end, when it came to Isolde's Transfiguration, the singer, Birgit Nilsson, clad in yellow, rose up like a new sun, while the light behind her, catching the aperture in the segment and turning it into a sickle crescent, was that of some alien moon's eclipse into eternal night.

Selective Bibliography

Two recent collections include important references to *Tristan*: the *Wagner Handbook*, edited by Müller and Wapnewski, translated by John Deathridge (Harvard, 1992), and *The Wagner Compendium*, edited by Barry Millington (London, 1992). A comprehensive bibliography will be found in the New Grove Dictionary of Opera (London, 1992). Elliott Zuckermann's *First Hundred Years of Wagner's Tristan* (New York, 1964) summarises many aspects of the opera; Joseph Kerman's *Opera as Drama* includes a chapter 'Opera as Symphonic Poem' (Faber, 1990); Robin Holloway's *Debussy and Wagner* (London, 1980) discusses *Tristan* and *Pelléas*. A short biography is by Barry Millington (London, 1992), while a longer one is by Martin Gregor Dellin (London, 1983); *A Documentary Study* by Barth, Mack and Voss (London, 1975) has illustrations and source documents in translation. Gottfried von Strassburg's myth (trans. S.T. Hatto) is in Penguin Classics, 1960.

Selective Discography
David Nice

The Beecham/Reiner set listed below is a composite of Covent Garden performances given under Reiner in May 1936 (part of the complete Reiner interpretation as issued on VAI) and under Beecham in June 1937. In both cases Melchior's Tristan can be heard complete; his role in excerpts is thus of secondary importance to two Isoldes otherwise under-represented — Helen Traubel on a CBS Masterworks 'Portrait' (CD46454) and the great Frida Leider, featured both on Preiser (89004) or in the second instalment of EMI's 'Wagner singing on record' (EMI CMS7 64008-2.2 — 4 CDs). Leider's *Liebestod* is not included on the EMI set, but there are alternative interpretations from Meta Seinemeyer and Germaine Lubin. Among countless orchestral Preludes and Liebestods, the swift and flexible approach of Richard Strauss conducting the Berlin Philharmonic in 1928 is of outstanding interest (Koch Legacy 3-7119 2III). All recordings listed are currently available on CD only; those asterisked are in mono.

Conductor	Reiner*	Reiner/Beecham* (see note)	Leinsdorf*	De Sabata* (with cuts)	Furtwängler*
Company/Orchestra	Royal Opera/LPO	Royal Opera/LPO	NY Met	La Scala	Royal Opera House Ch/Philharmonia
Date	1936	1936/37	1940	1951	1952
Tristan	Melchior	Melchior	Melchior	Lorenz	Suthaus
Isolde	Flagstad	Flagstad	Flagstad	Grob-Prandl	Flagstad
Brangäne	Kalter	Kalter/Klose	Thorborg	Cavelti	Thebom
King Mark	List	List/Nilsson	List	Nilsson	Greindl
Kurwenal	Janssen	Janssen	Hühn	S. Björling	Fischer-Dieskau
Sailor	Devereux	Jones	Marlowe	del Signore	Schock
Shepherd	Dua	Dua		della Pergola	Schock
Melot	Sale	Sale/Hitchin	Cehanovsky	Demetz	Evans
Steersman	Horsman	Horsman	Beattie	Campi	Davies
CD number	VAI Audio 1104-3 (3)	EMI CHS7 64037 (3)	Music and Arts CD647 (3)	Nuovo Era 2347-9 (3)	EMI CDS 7 473228 (4)

Conductor	*Solti*	*Böhm*	*Karajan*	*Bernstein*	*C. Kleiber*
Company/Orchestra	**Vienna Singverein/ VPO**	**Bayreuth**	**Deutsch Oper Ch/ BPO**	**Bavarian Radio SO & Ch**	**Leipzig Radio Ch/ Staatskapelle Dresden**
Date	1960	1966	1972	1981	1982
Tristan	Uhl	Windgassen	Vickers	Hofmann	Kollo
Isolde	Nilsson	Nilsson	Dernesch	Behrens	M. Price
Brangäne	Resnik	Ludwig	Ludwig	Minton	Fassbaender
King Mark	van Mil	Talvela	Ridderbusch	Sotin	Moll
Kurwenal	Krause	Wächter	Berry	Weikl	Fischer-Dieskau
Sailor	Kmentt	Schreier	Schreier	Moser	Büchner
Shepherd	Klein	Wohlfahrt	Schreier	Zednik	Dermota
Melot	Kozub	Heater	Weikl	Steinbach	Götz
Steersman	Kirschbichler	Nienstedt	Vantin	Grumbach	Hellmich
CD number	Decca/London 430 234 (4)	DG 419 889-2 (3)	EMI CMS 7 69319 2 (4)	DG 410 447-2 (4)	DG 413 315-2 (4)